Brighter Days Ahead

A Young Woman's Story of Fortitude Living With Obstetrical Brachial Plexus Injury

Wynnikka Matthews

"Brighter Days Ahead: A Young Woman's Story of Fortitude Living with Obstetrical Brachial Plexus Injury"

ISBN 978-1-7750428-0-8

Published by Wynnikka Matthews
www.wyninspires.com

Disclaimer:
All names and identifiable characteristics have been changed to protect the privacy and identities of individuals mentioned in this book, except for those who have given their expressed permission.

BRIGHTER DAYS AHEAD

"The last sonogram proved that I was perfectly fine. My mother did everything she could do to ensure I was a healthy, growing baby during her pregnancy, even though the pregnancy was already at-risk due to pre-existing health issues. I kicked and punched her with both arms and legs throughout her pregnancy. She felt every single one. And after having my younger siblings, she said I was the strongest kicker. She wanted a C-section, and she even dreamt about it months before my birth. However, when she asked about it at eight months pregnant, her doctor rejected her request and said she would "die on the table," because she was overweight. Both she and my father had put their trust in this doctor, because they felt that since I was going to be their firstborn child, after losing a baby boy two years prior, only he knew what was best for their baby..."

"Perseverance..."

"Resilience..."

"Maturity..."

"Motivation..."

PREFACE

This book is dedicated to my mother, Nicole Pearce. She had me working on this book since 2013, when she first told me the importance of getting my story out there. She gave me a notepad and pen, then told me to list everything I knew about my disability and what I've gone through— the bullying, how I get dressed, etcetera. And after listing everything, she got my laptop and told me to type it all out into an essay. Since then, I've been taking my time adding to it and expanding it into the book it is now.

My name is Wynnikka Matthews, and I am twenty-two years old. I not only wrote this book to motivate and inspire others by sharing my life experiences, but also to bring awareness to Brachial Plexus Birth Injury, also known as Obstetrical Brachial Plexus Injury (OBPI) or "Erb's Palsy." Many people tell me that their first thought about what must have happened to my right arm is that it was a birth defect that occurred within my mother's womb, before birth. However, this is not the case at all, hence the phrase "birth injury." In an interview I did about a scholarship I received a few years ago, the journalist referred to my arm as "deformed", a term I found to be offensive. I didn't actually read the newspaper article until well after it was published, and by that time, it was too late to contact him and ask him to make a change.

I believe there are many others of all ages who have also

suffered from this birth injury and are dealing with similar life experiences. Just like any other disability, OBPI not only affects the person who has it but may also affect those close to them, especially their immediate family. This particular disability isn't as widely known as most common physical disabilities. Hence, I am an advocate, and plan to raise awareness about it.

Support groups and services need to be put in place specifically designed to help those like myself who may feel alone with Obstetrical Brachial Plexus Injury outside of medical treatment. It isn't as hard to find information as it was in the past, especially with Google at our fingertips but when I search OBPI support, nothing in Canada comes up except for medical offices. Those with and without OBPI should learn about what it is. Pregnant women should be informed as well. We shouldn't be denied financial disability support and neither should our parents and caregivers, but some of us still do, even with the help of agencies. We need to be brought together like a family for moral support and to learn from each other's experiences whether it be in person or online. No child should feel how I felt growing up and no parent or caregiver should be left in the dark to go through what my parents went through.

> *"I am young*
> *I am a young woman*
> *I am a young woman of colour*
> *I am a young woman of colour with a disability, a disability that is not yet widely known but I am willing and ready to make that change!"*

FOOTPRINTS

One night a man had a dream. He dreamed he was walking along the beach with the Lord. Across the sky flashed scenes from his life. For each scene he noticed two sets of footprints in the sand; one belonging to him and the other to the Lord.

When the last scene of his life flashed before him, he looked back at the footprints in the sand. He noticed that many times along the path of his life there was only one set of footprints. He also noticed that it happened at the very lowest and saddest times of his life. This really bothered him and he questioned the Lord about it.

"Lord, you said that once I decided to follow you, you'd walk with me all the way. However, I noticed that during the most troublesome times of my life there was only one set of footprints. I don't understand why when I needed you most you would leave me."

The Lord replied, "my precious, precious child, I love you and I would never leave you during your times of trial and suffering, when you see only one set of footprints it was then that I carried you."

Carolyn Joyce Carty, American Poet © 1963

(Used with Permission of the Author)

ACKNOWLEDGEMENTS

Thank you mommy for handing me that pen and notepad in 2013, just before I graduated from high school, and telling me to begin writing my story. Thank you for believing in me! Here we are five years later and I really wish you were here to see the final product and enjoy it with the rest of the world! Thank you for teaching me the importance of getting my story out there because it will serve to educate, motivate, and inspire others.

"*No matter how long it takes Nika, make sure it gets done. It must be done!*", you'd say.

I love you and I miss you Mommy! Thank you to the rest of my family, my daddy, Winston Matthews, my younger brother Quan & sister Keys for how you've all shaped me into the person I am today! I love you all and each of you play a unique role in my life. No words can explain the amount of gratitude I extend towards you. Thank you for your continued encouragement, love and support.

Thank you Moy Fung for being such an amazing supporter and believer in my book being published. Thank you for being patient with my intensive inquisitiveness! Thank you for answering all the questions I had. Thank you for keeping me on my toes when it came to deadlines. Thank you for your compassion and reassurance when I had writer's block and began to worry. You can get incredibly busy sometimes, but you always made sure to find the time to get in touch with me. You are absolutely exceptional for the work you've done in helping me to bring this book to life!

Dr. Fred Mathews! I can say "thank you" a gazillion times and I'd still feel like it wouldn't be enough! I came to you with a 14 page essay in January, 2017 thinking my book was near done but in 1 year you helped me prepare and expand it to the fuller story it has become using a "life memory inventory". You always say you didn't do much but I don't think you realize how much you've done for me. Thank you for your kind and encouraging words. Thank you for all the time you took helping me. Thank you for making the time in between your busy schedule throughout the year. Thank you for your wisdom. Thank you for your contribution in making my book come to life. I'm glad you were a part of the journey with me! Thank you for going above and beyond for me and my dream. It's been a long time coming and the book is finally here!

Thank you Irwin Elman and The Office of the Provincial Advocate for Children and Youth for helping me to realize my passion for community-based work, advocating for others and working with children and youth! Thank you for all the wonderful opportunities you've allowed me to be a part of. Thank you for the new friends I've made through the office. Thank you for helping me to network with others and giving me the platform to speak and be a part of positive change. Thank you for allowing me to be a leader.

Thank you Lee Hon Bong for the gorgeous photo you captured of me that is now the cover of my book! The pose, the vibrant colours with the black background and my facial expression stood out to me. I knew from the moment I saw it that it would be the one!

Thank you Carolyn Joyce Carty, American Poet, for responding to my message within an hour of receiving it! I was so shocked at how fast you got back to me. Thank you for allowing me to include your wonderful "Footprints" poem in my book to show others something that helped my family and I through tough times for many, many years.

Thank You Kerri-Ann Haye-Donawa, Manager at Conclusio House Publishing, for carefully editing my book. Your hard work is greatly appreciated!

Thank you to everyone who believed in my book and believed that it'll truly serve its purpose in inspiring others and changing lives. You've helped to keep me going and helped me to believe in myself especially at times when I didn't.

Thank you to the doctor who delivered me. Thank you to those who've tested me, tormented me, knocked me down, mocked me, isolated me and made me hate myself at a point in time. To those who judged me based on my physical appearance before they even took the time to get to know me, to those who still make fun of my disability in public and take pictures or videos for laughs-I forgive you. You've contributed to and continue to contribute to my abundance of strength. I'll come out on top because I was born a winner. I was born a leader. All the pressure and hardship from you along with the gentle care and shaping from those genuinely looking out for my best interest, formed this diamond.

Cheers to you all!

TABLE OF CONTENTS

FOREWORD

As I read *"Brighter Days Ahead"* it occurred to me that the story it tells is really about two women. It is the story of strength, courage, determination and most of all love.

I met Wynnikka years ago – decades really. I knew her Mother even before Wynnikka was a glimmer in her Mother's eye. I can attest to the fierce determination of her Mom. It was some kind of kismet when as Ontario's Child Advocate Wynnikka came to visit me. Now a young woman she showed me an article about herself in a Toronto newspaper. She told me about the loss she suffered and about her hopes and dreams. I saw her Mother in her. When my staff eventually hired her as an Amplifier at our Office I was not surprised that they saw in her the same qualities that I saw.

When Wynnikka, with great humility, handed me "her story" she told me it was about how she coped with a "disability". She said she "hoped it would help others overcome the barriers that they would face" and that it "might make a difference". It certainly will make a difference. Her story documents her childhood, adolescent and emerging adulthood struggles to daily meet the challenges she has faced and pushed past. It is a meticulous account. It is inspiring.

As if this was not enough, I learned more from "Brighter Days Ahead" about the mother-daughter relationship. Wynnikka looks to her mother as a great source of wisdom and strength. I learned that they both grew together through their relationship and that they offered support to each other in what seemed an unsaid way. It is a powerful reminder of the importance of our relationships with our children which nurtures the caregiver and those being cared for.

I learned about grieving and loss and how one copes.

I learned about the transition for young people becoming actors in the world. I learned about school, bullying, health care, employment, and hope. I learned about love. Wynnikka is not shy about expressing it in her way including the struggle to love herself.

This book is remarkable. If you are holding it I encourage you to read with an open heart and mind. It is the spirit in which it was written that is so powerful. I thank Wynnikka for this gift to all of us.

Irwin Elman
Provincial Advocate
Office of the Provincial Advocate for
Children and Youth, Ontario Canada

CHAPTER 1

First Breath

I was perfectly fine in my mother's womb. My mother did everything she could to ensure that I was a healthy, growing baby, despite her pre-existing health conditions, such as being overweight. I was moving, kicking, and punching her with all my might, she said. The very last sonogram, better known as an ultrasound, showed that I was perfectly fine. She requested a caesarean section, on multiple occasions, but her doctor declined. She even dreamt about having one and felt as though she should follow through with it. However, he told her she didn't know what she was talking about and said that she would put her life at risk and die on the table, because she was overweight.

When she was in labour, they realized something was wrong, but the doctor did not go and ask for further assistance, he decided to deal with it on his own, just him, the nurse, and my father in the room. There wasn't an emergency C-section room set up either, just in case something went wrong. He just told her to push harder and began yanking on my head and twisting it. He also used forceps, which left abrasions—big bumps that oozed in the two areas the forceps squeezed—on my head. The nurse also repeatedly pushed down on my mother's lower stomach. All of these steps that he took are believed to be medical malpractices. The end result was that fragile nerves were ripped completely from my spinal cord. I believe the doctor might not have had any experience with a situation like this, and panicked, thus committing medical malpractice where I became the victim. There are other ways in which he could've handled the situation to prevent the injury from occurring but, unfortunately, he did things his way. The thought makes me angry and frustrated sometimes, because I wonder what my life would've been like had he just listened to my mother's intuition and either agreed to complete a C-section or send her to the other hospital where she had wished to deliver me. Eventually, I had surgery to mend the damaged nerves; but after that, my parents did not trust service providers with my care, other than my grandmother who was working at the children's hospital at the time.

My disability is called Obstetrical Brachial Plexus Injury (brake-e-al plex-us). The injury is physically noticeable, with my right arm being partially paralyzed and limp. My right hand, when I'm standing up, also appears to be turned inwards and "clawed." My right arm feels significantly cooler than my left arm due to the lack of circulation, and sometimes causes pain that can be unbearable at times. The surgery was unsuccessful and, unfortunately, wasn't able to repair any of the damaged nerves due to the severity of the injury. Every nerve was damaged from C5 down to T1. The surgeon made an incision on the back of both my ankles, where the scars are still present, and took nerves out that he believed wouldn't be needed. He then made another incision, over my right collar bone and a bit up on the right side on my neck to mend the nerves taken from my ankles with the ones that were damaged; this scar is also still visible today.

When I was a toddler I had many seizures. The very first one I had was in my father's arms at the age of two. I had an extremely high fever, and my parents were in the doctor's waiting room when my eyes rolled back, and I began shaking violently. My parents started panicking because it was unexpected and they didn't know what was happening to their baby girl. Every time I had a high fever, I would have a seizure. One day it was really bad, and 9-1-1 was called from home. I had a seizure that lasted more than five minutes. When the paramedics arrived, they said I would be fine. A half hour after they had left, my parents called 9-1-1 again, and the same paramedics came back to rush me to the hospital. The doctor had suggested I be put in an ice bath to help cool down the fever, but my mother declined. She did, however, agree to have me patted down with a cool, damp cloth, and that helped. I grew out of seizures by the age of five, and haven't had one since.

Brachial Plexus Injury affects both sides of my body. On Monday, June 30, 2014, I found out that I also have Scoliosis, a curved spine. This diagnosis helped my family to understand why I had been having back problems and breathing issues. This troubled me because I could not understand why any of the practitioners who had examined me in the past had never brought this to my parents' attention. Every time I complained about my back or breathing issues, doctors would tell me that I just needed to lose weight, then the pain would subside and my breathing would go back to normal. I started having serious back pain, to the point where it kept me up at night, and my family doctor finally decided to take a look at my back. He said my back looked curved and that I needed an x-ray. They found that I have a curved spine that needs to be taken care of. Had this been noticed earlier on in my life, things could have been done to correct my curved spine, like wearing a brace or having scoliosis surgery to help prevent my spine from continuing to curve.

After my doctor appointment that day, my parents and I went home, and my mom started doing my hair. While sitting down, I noticed something while holding my arm out, so I asked my mother about it. I had never asked her before, and she just looked at me with a worried expression on her face and called my dad over. They held out both their arms, and I was so confused. They told me to hold out my left arm and said, "Nika, look. You see the difference in our arms in comparison to your left arm? You have Brachial Plexus Injury in your left arm too."

I looked up at them in disbelief and yelled, "What?"

Then Dad explained, "Well, at seven months old, before your surgery, the surgeon told us he'd only focus on your right arm, only because that's where most of the damage was, and he assured us the nerves would regenerate themselves in your left arm, but the rotation of your forearm is a bit different."

I felt my face getting hot, and mom looked down at me and began crying. "The only reason why we didn't tell you all these years is because we knew in our hearts what you were capable of, and we didn't want you to know you had a disability in both arms, then use it as an excuse not to try certain things and push yourself. It was one of the hardest things we ever had to do, but look at who and what you are now."

They thought I'd be mad at them, but I was actually very grateful that they did what they did and stuck with the decision to keep it from me until I was old enough to understand why. I screamed, "It's not fair!" and fell to the floor. I started crying, because I couldn't believe my delivering practitioner had done all of this to me, and it could've all been avoided. I'm worried about my future because my left arm over compensates everyday and becomes fatigued. I still try to do everything I can, before asking for help, but BPI and nerve damage still exists in my left arm, so I do have to take it easy.

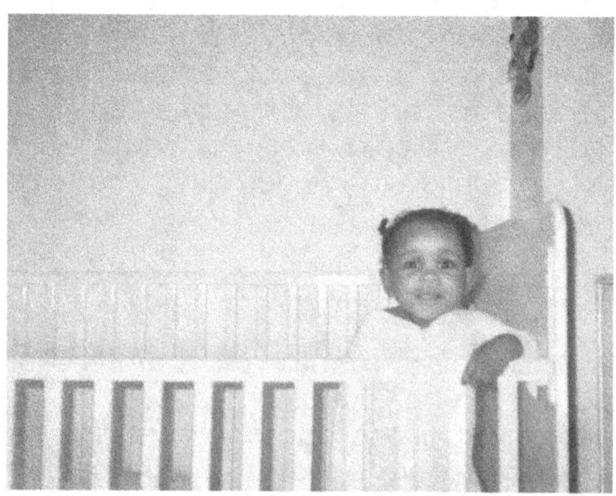

That is me at about two years old posing so adorably for the camera in my onesie

CHAPTER 2

Realization

My very first challenge was to learn to crawl, something that typically comes naturally to a developing infant. On my hands and knees, I'd attempt to crawl forward, but the movement to go forward was disrupted because I could not push my right arm forward to support the front right side of my body. My right knee was also too weak to pull me forward while supporting my weight. I'd fall forward if my parents weren't holding out their arms to catch me. This absolutely broke my parents' hearts, especially when I cried, because they could see that I was trying. Eventually, I learned to crawl in my own unique way, but when I swung my right arm forward and landed my weight on it, I hurt my right wrist. I began to use tables and chairs to hold myself up, first to stand and then to walk. I taught myself to stand up and sit down carefully using my legs and leaning on my left arm or using no arms at all.

My favourite thing to do as a baby was to bounce in my swing in the door frame. I would never get bored of doing it; I was a swinging, jumping, laughing, happy, healthy baby. I always had strong legs, so this was like involuntarily toning my legs as early as I could. My first word was not "Mamma" or "Dada," it was "No!". Every question they asked me, the answer was "No!" And if anyone tried to get me to share my belongings the answer was still "No!". I laugh when my parents tell me about this, because I now find it hard to say "No" to other people. I'm always willing to lend a helping hand, sometimes making compromises and sacrifices of my own just to make the situation best for everyone. The Dr. Seuss Book Collection helped me to develop my vocabulary. All the rhymes and tongue twisters really had me going. Not only did I enjoy them when I was younger, but I also enjoyed reading them all to my younger siblings and laughing at all the humour within them.

During my toddler stage, I slept in a crib in the same room as my parents. However, I'd wake up way before them. They told me that to get their attention I'd stand up, hold on to the bars of the crib, and shake it with all my toddler might until it rattled. If they didn't get up right away, I'd continue with my shenanigans and add some screaming and crying, until one of them got up and let me out.

My mother used to tell me that when she'd take me out for a stroll, people used to come up to her and say how beautiful I was. Then they would notice my arm and show concern by asking what happened to me. Some of these people even offered money to help, because they felt really bad and wondered why my parents hadn't sued the "pants off" of the doctor responsible. However, my parents never accepted money from anyone for what had happened to me; instead, they'd kindly decline the offers and thank those kind people for showing concern, while reassuring them that they were trying their best.

When I was younger, I was always determined to try anything. I was oblivious to the fact that I had a disability when it came time to play, because my parents never placed any physical limits on me. Playing with toys was fine, but when it came to playing video games with controllers that required the use of two hands, I often became frustrated at the fact that I couldn't play with two hands. My father couldn't stand to see me upset, so he'd put one hand behind his back and found a way to play and touch all the buttons using just one hand; then he showed me how to do it, too. I found myself straining my left wrist sometimes, but I honestly didn't care, because all I wanted to do was play. I had a Nintendo 64, and all I ever played was Mario's World. Sometimes I hated that I had to play the game differently than others, but I still made sure to play it.

I was about two years old when I wrote my full name by myself with my left hand. I was sitting on the floor beside the coffee table and took a pen and began writing my name by myself on an important envelope instead of on a scrap piece of paper. I didn't get in trouble, because my parents were proud that I had finally figured out how to write my name by myself. I feel that in some way I may have naturally been right-handed. I say this because I remember sometimes wanting to use my right hand, or subconsciously reaching with my right hand then adjusting to use my left hand.

When I was growing up, my parents held a birthday party for me every year. My favourite memory is of my second birthday party, which was Barney-themed. Most of my and my siblings' birthday parties took place at Chuckie Cheese's; it was our most favourite place to go. A lot of family members and family friends would come to celebrate, and every party was one to remember.

I remember being at a doctor's office and receiving my first

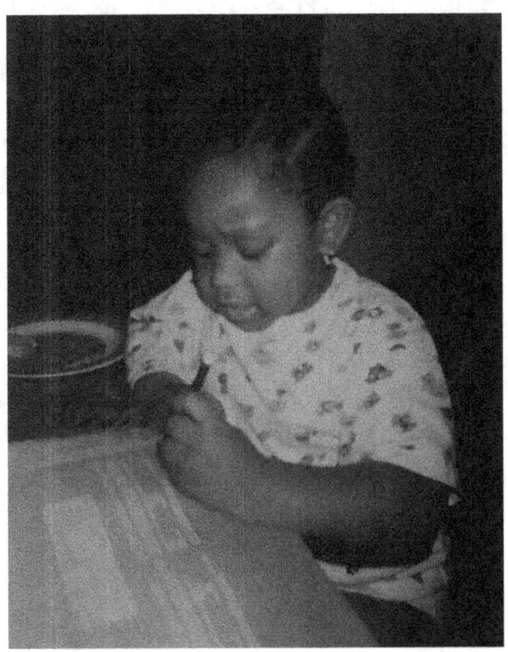

This is the picture of me writing my full name on that important envelope

hand brace. It was colourful and had Velcro straps. Because of the way my hand would point down from the wrist, my wrist hurt, but the splint in the brace would hold my hand straight and align it with my forearm to ease the pain. Since I've grown out of it, I haven't had another one until recently, when I began physiotherapy and it was suggested that I get a new one.

When my brother was a few months old, and I was about two-and-a-half, we shared a room. I remember always finding a way to jump into his crib with him after we were left alone for nap time, because looking at him through the bars of the crib just wasn't enough for me. In our room there were these two small, plastic, resin chairs at a small workstation table. I would take one and place it against the crib. I would then climb up, placing my two feet between two of the crib bars, as my baby brother would smile and giggle, watching my every move. I managed to prop my right elbow over the top railing and lean to my right while raising my left foot up over the railing, flipping myself into the crib without ever hurting the baby. I went in there and pressed the buttons on the musical mobile so he could see the animals light up, move, and make lullaby sounds. The funniest part of it all was that I knew how to hide the evidence of how I got into the crib. I did so by sticking my left arm through the bars from inside the crib, reaching for the top of the chair, then swinging it as far as I could forward then backward towards me, then down under the crib so they couldn't figure out how I got in there. When my parents came into the room, they would find me in the crib with him playing, and they would take pictures. One day my mom wanted to catch me in the act. So, instead of leaving us to fall asleep for nap time, she came and checked to see what I was doing, literally every five minutes, with her Polaroid camera in hand ready to go. Of course, I did not go to sleep right away, but rather began the process of getting into my brother's crib. My mom told me her jaw dropped the whole time she watched me, as she could not believe what she was seeing. She crept up behind me, taking pictures, and as soon as I flipped into the crib, she said "gotcha!" and my facial expression was priceless. I still have the photo of my reaction to this day. It is funny to stare at and remember.

When I was about three years old, I became adventurous, and every chance I got, I'd climb up on the loveseat in the living room to slap around the vertical blinds. We lived downtown in a condo, so one of my favourite things to do was look out the window, because we had a pretty close view of the CN Tower and it truly amazed me. My parents had this suede, deep off-black couch with faded splashes of blue and pink streaks. It was leaned against the wall next to the living room window. Every chance I got, when no one was looking, I'd bolt over to the loveseat, jump on it, stand up facing the window, put one foot up on an arm of the chair to hoist myself up higher, and begin slapping the blinds back and forth, and back and forth. The noise would startle my parents, and they would run out from wherever they were for a brief moment, whether they were in the kitchen, bedroom, or in the middle of using the washroom, because they thought I had fallen or hurt myself, but instead they found me giggling at the noise of the swaying blinds clashing against each other.

I was very creative, especially building with Lego blocks. Not the tiny ones, but the "Duplo" version that was built for the age group of one-and-a-half to five years old. I had a humongous set in a bin that had a triple Lego platform to build from. Out of all my toys, it was my favourite to play with. I would build the sculptures super-high and balanced. I rarely ever had a tower I built fall back on me. I found it fascinating. I used to try and mimic the build of the CN Tower and the Rogers Centre, because every time I looked out the window, I saw them. I played with building blocks until I was about twelve years old, and it was always fun to me; I never got bored of it. I used to always show my younger brother and sister how to build like me. I also enjoyed stacking playing cards into a pyramid. My love for building and stacking began to get me into trouble after some time. I started stacking cans way too high, and I got warned about doing so until one day the stack fell back on me. I hurt a few of my left fingers and my wrist, but I don't remember the pain lasting for more than a day. One of my parents' favourite Jamaican sayings is, "Who nuh hear must feel." In translation, it means if you were warned about the risk in doing something, and you still proceeded, you are bound to get hurt; a kind of "I told you so." This didn't necessarily mean in a physical way, however.

Whenever I was left to watch my favourite shows and drink my "baba" (baby bottle or sippy cup) while my parents completed chores around the house, I was put in my car seat. After a while, I'd twist and push myself until I slipped out of the car seat, only to go get into something I wasn't supposed to. My parents couldn't understand how I didn't harm myself, especially my right arm, while doing these things, since I had to lean more to my right because only my upper left side was being supported by my left arm, hand and wrist.

My father had a funny way of showing me when things were dangerous to do, or to touch, by being overly dramatic when demonstrating why it was dangerous. Case in point, I had a silver Barney necklace that I loved to play with. I was about four years old. There weren't any cover plates to childproof electrical outlets at that time, so, of course, at some point I found it quite interesting to go and play with them. I thought it would be fun and fascinating to try to stick my silver Barney that was on the chain into the socket. I didn't actually get a chance to stick Barney into the socket, because my father caught me right before I did it and picked me up away from the outlet. He asked me to hand him the chain, and I'll never forget what unfolded next. He took the chain and pretended he was being electrocuted. I remember seeing him shaking violently on the floor with his hand still holding the Barney chain near the outlet. I started crying, and when he got up to pick me up, I was definitely beyond terrified to do that again. From that day, do you think I ever put anything anywhere close to a socket unless it was a plug with two prongs or more? Never! Thanks, Dad.

There is a picture of me, at four years old, climbing up on a chair that was turned to face the kitchen sink, attempting to do dishes. We had these purple hanging beads in the doorway of the kitchen, and one of my parents took a picture of me, from behind the beads, wearing pull-ups and a white t-shirt with two ponytails up on the chair, playing in the sink.

I remember when my brother was about three years old I began to notice something different about myself. How come he could wave both arms around and wash both his hands? I started to hit my hand and hurt myself because I didn't like my right hand. I began to question why I couldn't move that arm. I noticed that I couldn't move my right arm at all like him. I began to hate my arm, and I showed the signs to my parents by getting upset easily when I was clapping. I started hitting my right arm with my left fist. Sometimes I was caught taking safety scissors, trying to go at my fingers on my right hand, trying to cut them. I got in some serious trouble for doing that when I did eventually get caught. I didn't feel as if they were a part of me, and my mom would sternly tell me to "stop it." As I got older, she reminded me of how much having to deal with that made them cry, but not in front of me.

I was five years old when I received my favourite purple bike with training wheels on it. One day, I jumped up and demanded that my father take the training wheels off. They said I kept seeing other kids older and bigger than me riding their bikes without training wheels at the park, and so I didn't want them anymore. I no longer wanted to look like a "baby." My mom told him not to, but he argued that if I felt I was ready to be a big girl to let me try; and if he saw that I couldn't ride without them, then he would put them back on. It was a cloudy day when they brought my brother and me to the park by our school, and my father and I walked my bike into the school field so that even if I fell, I'd fall into the grass. At the farthest end of the field, facing the direction where Mom was sitting cheering me on with Quan, I sat on my bike with my feet on both pedals and my hands on the handles, while Dad placed one hand on my right handle over my hand and his other hand on the seat. He told me to keep pedaling while he held onto the bike. I kept pedaling as fast as I could, and when we got halfway, I heard Mom yelling for me to keep pedaling, while holding Quan. And Dad, running behind me, kept telling me to keep pedaling fast. He let go of the handle, held onto the back of the seat for two more spins of the pedal, then let go completely. I was riding my bike.

As I was getting closer to Mom, it began to rain, and they were so proud. We went home in a hurry, but I had learned how to ride my bike. I outgrew that bike fast, and I remember getting my second favourite bike that was purple, just like my first bike, but with silver and blue writing. It was an adult-sized bike, with the seat at the lowest setting, that grew with me. Because I was left-handed and could only steer my bike with my left hand, mom and dad had gotten the left and right brake lines on my bike switched, so that when I pulled the left brake handle, it would stop my back tire instead of the front tire like other bikes. Therefore, I was never allowed to ride anyone else's bike in the park when I went outside. However, there was a time when I just didn't listen and, again, I felt it. I rode one of my friends' bikes fast around the park, and pulled the brake, but used my feet to assist in stopping. The second time, I guess I forgot to use my feet to stop the bike safely without it lifting off the ground from the front, and when I pulled the handle while both my feet were still on the pedals, the bike flipped over forward, and I fell right off the bike. I didn't sustain any serious injuries, but a few scrapes on my knees from the pavement and the handles hurting one of my sides during the flip and fall taught me a big lesson.

CHAPTER 3

Growing Pains

My parents were my personal support workers and physiotherapists, especially when I used to wake up many nights with a cramping pain in my right arm. They never got help or training but stayed up late nights and took many days off work to stay and massage the painful areas, do arm movement rotations, find comfortable ways for me to sleep without being in pain, etcetera. I never started physiotherapy until late 2016, just after I turned twenty-one. Although it is expensive, and I have never gotten treatment since I was very young, I decided to just go ahead and start it, because I found myself in too much pain. My parents always helped me to get dressed, but as I got older, they'd also find unique ways of helping me to care for myself when they weren't around. Many times, they'd try to do certain tasks with their right arm behind their backs to try to teach me how to care for myself with my left arm alone, and how to use other parts of my body to assist with getting daily tasks done. They hated to see me use my teeth to assist with tasks, and so did my dentist. I should note that as much as I used my teeth to tug and pull on clothing and ties, I'm so grateful that in the process of doing so, I haven't injured any of my teeth or gums. To this day, I still use my teeth to compensate for not being able to use my right arm, because it's the only way I know how, and it also comes naturally to me. Many of the things that I used to get a lot of help with, I can now do with accommodations. Some things do take me longer to complete due to my limitations, but I still try to get them done.

Because I'm always striving for independence, people often

ask me why I never just ask them for help. I hate the feeling of someone feeling sorry for me. My brother and my sister have become my little Personal Service Workers (PSWs) as well to help with some small, everyday tasks that most people "autopilot" themselves to complete without thinking. My friends also help when I'm with them; either I ask for their assistance or they automatically start helping me, without me having to ask, even with things I've already accommodated myself with. I hate always asking someone for help, because sometimes I feel like I'm a bother to them. I don't want to feel that way, so I refrain from asking more often than not. No one ever really had a problem with helping me, but I'd rather just sit there and figure out a way to get it done myself than to ask for help. Sometimes when I decide to give up, because I really cannot do the task on my own while using the accommodations I've tried with just one hand, I then ask for assistance from others. There are times when no one I know is around to help me, and if I seriously do need to get the task done, I will swallow my pride and ask for help from a stranger.

When at home alone, I will attempt to do something by myself, but if I can't do it, or if doing it is putting me at risk for harm, then I'm left with no choice but to sit there and wait until someone comes home to assist me. An example would be something as simple as boiling water in a big pot that has two handles. There is no way I can lift a medium-large pot full of water and strain rice or noodles without assistance. There have been times, of course, when I have attempted to so, on my own. I would put on an oven mitten on both hands and try to hold the hot pot. However, because there's an imbalance in supporting the hot pot, as soon as I picked it up it would begin to slip out of my hands. If I moved super-fast after picking it up, there was a chance I'd make it to the sink without dropping the pot. Sometimes I would make it to the sink, and other times it would slip, and I'd let it drop back onto the burner. I'd always get into trouble for this, because I should've asked for help, when all I wanted was to be completely independent. Holding anything with my right arm requires the full strength of my entire right arm, so in the process it usually puts a strain on my shoulders.

My mom used to say to me, "You know, Nika, you can't keep ignoring the fact that you have a disability, and keep trying to do everything on your own. You are putting yourself at risk, and you can really injure yourself. For example, whenever you go to the grocery store by yourself, instead of lifting the case of water and hurting your left arm and your back in the process, just ask for help! Ask the cashier to call for a carry-out, so an employee can bring the cases for you. I understand you don't want people to feel sorry for you, but you need to get all the assistance you can get, and stop rejecting when others offer to do so."

After a while, I began to take heed by asking for, and accepting, the help I could get. I still do try to keep the asking to a minimum, because I feel as if I don't want to bother anyone to help me, although I may need the help. I do want to venture out and live on my own, but I may not ever have the chance to live entirely on my own, because someone needs to be around to help me with some daily tasks. I may have to jump right from the nest (home) to getting married and living with my husband, so I can have the help I need. Having a support person to come in and check on me every now and then would be an option as well, especially when I have children. I do not have a major problem with doing either of these things; it's just that my independence has been limited for the rest of my life.

I believe I was about eight years old when I made the following mistake that left a permanent scar on my leg. I was super curious and began to get into things I shouldn't have. I saw a box with razors in the washroom and decided that I'd shave my legs. I really don't know why I decided to do this, because I had not one strand of hair on my legs. I wet the razor and began pulling it up my leg, and I pulled too hard at my left thigh and made a three-inch vertical cut up my thigh right above my knee. I dropped the razor and screamed out for my mom repeatedly, until she came. She found me "cow bawling" with blood dripping down my leg, making a small pool of blood at my feet. She said, "Nika! What were you thinking shaving your legs?" She managed to laugh a little and ran to get some first-aid material to clean me up and treat the cut. I remember crying and begging her not to call 9-1-1 on me, which made her laugh. Then she turned to me and said, "Who nuh hear, must feel." I heard this saying every time I got into something I wasn't supposed to, after being warned beforehand, and I either got into trouble or got hurt.

The following are simple daily tasks that my parents had to teach themselves so they could teach me how to do them in accommodative ways—I find that these are more time consuming and challenging. I know it's hard to envision how I do all the following things for myself. Don't worry, you're not alone. Many people I try to explain it to without showing them how – become very puzzled because they have to see it to believe it.

Brushing My Teeth — Sometimes I'd hold the bottom of my manual toothbrush in my mouth and use my left hand to screw open the toothpaste and squeeze it onto the toothbrush while I'm still holding it in my mouth. I'd then put the toothpaste back down on the counter and begin brushing my teeth. Sometimes I'd push my toothbrush into the grip of my right hand while I put the toothpaste on. But I find it so annoying this way, because there are so many times when after I'm done putting the toothpaste on the toothbrush, and while putting the toothpaste tube back on the counter, the toothbrush falls or flips over, causing the dab of toothpaste on it to fall off, and then I have to repeat the process. I don't really like this way, but my dentist suggests that I try to limit the things I use my teeth for to compensate for my right arm, because it isn't doing any good for my teeth. I understand that, but I get so annoyed sometimes that I just go back to the way I'm most comfortable with. Of course, it would be easier to just squeeze toothpaste onto my tongue first but... just... "no bueno." To floss, I'd use those easy flossing sticks with a pick at the end. This way is super-easy, because it is one-handed.

Showering — I hold the loofa or washcloth under my right arm, closer in the middle of my right forearm, pressing the loofa or washcloth against my right ribcage or stomach area. I then hold the bottle of body wash in my right hand, pour some onto the loofa, then proceed to exfoliate my skin. The only thing is that scrubbing my left arm is a bit awkward sometimes, because I have to hold the loofa between my knees for a quick second and proceed with scrubbing.

Zipping up a Zipper – Kids used to laugh and mock the way I tried to zip up my jacket and it really upset me in my early years of elementary school. In order to zip up a jacket, a person has to hold both ends with both hands, and for me that wasn't possible for years. Until I got the hang of accommodating myself, I always needed help. When I was in grade two, and it was time to get ready for recess, I was often the last one to get ready. It took me so long to get everything on by myself. Sometimes the teacher would find me still getting on my things even ten minutes after being sent to my cubby; then she would offer to help. Mind you, recess was only fifteen minutes, so my recess was always cut short at that young age, to just five or ten minutes. After a few months, my teacher for that grade two class offered to help me get on my gloves, hat, scarf, and to help zip up my jacket almost every recess. Of course, I got bullied for this; kids would call me a baby because I needed an adult to help me put on my clothes. By the time I got outside, it still felt like I barely had any time to play.

One day during the winter—I actually cannot remember the specific details of this day, but my mother always reminds me of it, because it makes her furious and sad, no matter how old I get—the temperature was just below zero and it was almost time for our first recess of the day. All the kids were sent to their cubbies to get on their winter outdoor clothing by a substitute teacher. However, because the teacher had only known us for a few hours, he didn't have time to catch on to the fact that I had a disability, that it took longer for me to get ready, and that I needed help getting on my outdoor winter clothing. He rushed me outside along with the other kids, and the only thing I managed to do was haul on my right mitten over my right hand. My boots and snow pants were on, but I was wearing no scarf, no hat on my head, and I couldn't get on my left mitten, because at that time I did not know how to use my teeth to assist in getting it on my hand. I was outside for the majority of the recess in below zero weather, not dressed properly, making me susceptible to getting sick. I was absolutely oblivious to this, and so I didn't complain about being cold, nor did I ask for help from anyone, especially because I didn't have friends at the time to play with and I didn't want to be seen asking a teacher for help in front of everyone and get made fun of. That is what my mom said I told her when she asked me why I didn't ask anyone for help, and it made her even angrier. She told me that the situation made her cry, but she never did so in front of me.

One of our neighbours happened to be walking her daughter to school late when she spotted me outside. I was not friends with her daughter because she was one of the children who bullied me the worst, and I straight up hated her. She walked right up to me with no regard for the school policy that said parents weren't allowed to interact with other children on school property, unless they had already checked in with the office. She said "Hi" to me, and I said "Hi" to her, then she just reached for my zipper and zipped up my jacket for me and put on my hoodie. I thanked her, then ran off to go play. After signing her daughter in at the office, she went straight to my house to tell my mom what she couldn't believe she had witnessed with her own eyes. She was very upset and told my mom everything she saw and what she did. What made them both really angry was how not one of the yard duty teachers noticed that a young child wasn't dressed at all for the below zero weather.

My mother got dressed, then marched right over to the school to sign me out early. As she was waiting for me to come down from my class, she started yelling at the principal in anger, while crying about what happened, then left with me. She called the principal after coming home and calming down, and apologized to him for releasing her anger on him, and assured him that it wasn't directed towards him. However, she wanted him to do something about what had happened or else she'd write a letter to the superintendent of the school. I don't remember if that issue got resolved or not. Growing up, my mother taught me a valuable lesson. She was the most polite, most loving, most welcoming, most warmhearted, most generous, and the gentlest lady anyone would ever meet, but if anyone ever crossed her, they'd regret it soon. She was very passionate if something negative happened to her children, or family as a whole. The real Jamaican—"One Gyal Soldier", "Yardie" (from back home)—would jump out, and when she was done, some people were left in shock or crying. No one could ever try and tell her about herself without being told off and having no choice but to walk away in silence. When those people saw her again, she'd make amends with them, exchange apologies, and laugh like nothing ever happened. I don't know if it was the whole Libra and "keeping balance in all aspects of life" thing, but she was quick to forgive and make amends with others. I admire her for that, along with the many other things I admire about her.

After the incident, my father taught me a clever way of getting on my outdoor winter clothes. If it was pants, I'd sit on a chair or on the floor and hold the pants open in front of me. Then I'd stick my right leg in first then my left leg, and reach down and pull up the right side then the left side, alternating sides until the pants reached my knees. I'd stand up and repeat the same thing until the pants were over my hips. In an accommodative way, I'd button the button or close the hook first with just my left hand. When putting on my jacket, I'd zip up the zipper a little bit, lay it out flat on a carpet facing up, step into the jacket, stick my feet through, stick my right arm in first, then my left arm, and then zip it all the way up, get up and get going. Sometimes this still took quite long, so my father zipped my jacket up a little bit and stuck a baby pin at the bottom so that the zipper would never become unhooked. All I had to do was zip it down, step into it like pants—since it was still hooked—use my left hand to assist my right arm through the right sleeve of the jacket and pull the right shoulder of the jacket over my right shoulder. Then I'd push my left arm through on the left sleeve of the jacket, reach back and put up my hood, then zip the zipper and go on outside. For a sweater or small jacket with a zipper, I would use my right hand, push the bottom of the right side into my right hand to hold into place, bracing it against my body, then use my left hand to interlock the zipper onto the right side until it clicks. I'd then use my front teeth or right hand to hold the interlocked zipper in place, and use my left hand to pull up the zipper, and gradually let my teeth or right hand go of the bottom of the zip. As old as I am, up until a few weeks before she passed away, my mom still cried about the one time our neighbour saw me outside at recess with my jacket zipped down and no one came to my aid to help me zip it up. I could have caught a bad cold; I was freezing without even realizing it.

I don't really like the winter season due to the shorter days, snow and cold, just like anyone else who dislikes winter. But don't get me wrong, I enjoy throwing random, surprise snowballs at friends and family members. I also enjoy the blankets of snow during or after a winter storm in the evening when the sky has a purplish hue; it looks absolutely beautiful. Nonetheless, I hate the cold. A lot of the cramping in my arm comes from poor circulation, but then the cold and wind-chill makes it so much worse for me. Sometimes the pain is so unbearable that I have to take my right arm out of my sleeve and stick it inside my shirt for skin-to-skin contact to warm it up, or bundle up with extra layers of clothing. This does happen to me most nights when I go to bed. There were many times, a couple times a week, when I'd accidently fall asleep on my right arm and wake up in the middle of the night with a cramping, numbing pain. In fear of losing my right arm due to poor circulation, I'd sit up, even half asleep, and lightly slap or rub the heck out of my right forearm and hand, or run it under warm water, which I think does absolutely nothing but soothe the pain. Eventually, I'd start to feel the blood flowing back into my arm and fingers then go back to bed.

As my siblings grew older they started noticing my disability more. They would see me struggling with certain things and tell me they hated the doctor that did this to me. I would tell them that "hate" is a strong word and not to say it. Things happen, and I'm still trying to live the life I want to live the best way I can. Of course, I didn't deserve this, and he should've taken better care. I also told them that I have the love, support, and help of my family. I'm very protective of them and they are my little bodyguards. I love them, and I don't want them to feel hatred when they look at my arm and think of the doctor. I want them to be forgiving and to remember all I've achieved, regardless of my disability. I want them to see strength, resilience, perseverance, and have faith in a bright future for me. I am not doomed. Sure, there are things in life that I want to be and things I want to do, but I've had to have the strength to adjust my goals and plans, and keep moving forward. And you know what? I'm doing well.

CHAPTER 4

Self-Care

I used, and still use, my teeth a lot to help complete my daily tasks. I've been doing it for years and I'm grateful that nothing bad has ever happened to my teeth while doing any of these things.

Putting on a shirt/bra — I first hook the bra, then put it over my head completely, always putting my right arm through first then putting my left arm up and through.

Putting on socks with one hand — I open the sock with two left fingers, put it over my big toe, hold it in place over my toe and stretch it over my whole foot, then pull it by the ankle over the rest of my foot. Repeat for the next foot.

Putting on pants/underwear — I push both legs through and pull up the sides by pulling up a little bit on each side and switching sides until the pants are all the way up.

Putting on a hat with one hand (for example, a beanie winter hat) — I put one side of the opening over my forehead, brace my forehead with the front of the hat against a wall, and pull the back of the hat over the rest of my head. Because the beanie is stretchy, and I don't want to look silly putting it on in public places like school, I'll hide in a bathroom stall and use my teeth to grip the front of the hat and pull the rest backwards. With hats like a sunhat or "dad's hat," I use a wall, but in the opposite direction. I stand with my back against the wall, place the back of the hat on the back of my head first, press the back of my head against the wall to secure the hat in place, while pulling the rest up to the front of my head. It can take me a little longer sometimes to get the whole thing properly over my head, but I still get the job done.

Buckling a belt or buttoning up clothing — I usually push the belt all the way through the loops of my pants before putting them on. After putting on my pants, I stick the belt through the buckle on the left side, and pull as hard as I can to the right to tighten. I use my right hand to hold the belt in place with as much strength as possible then slide the rest of the belt through the loops until it's snug.

Buttons on pants — I first hold myself against a wall on my right side. I then pull each side of the waistband together as much as possible, overlapping the button hole over the button with my left hand, and pushing the button through the hole with my fingers (the same goes for buttoning up a sweater or jacket with buttons). I don't always stand against a wall; I use whatever is convenient for me at that moment. I can lay on my bed, or on my back if necessary. If my pants give way for a stretch, I can just pull both sides of the waistband together with my left index finger, middle finger & thumb.

Washing hands – "Although your right hand isn't dirty, still wash with both of your hands. It's a part of you. Go back and wash both your hands!" my mom would remind me. Sometimes when I was younger, I'd forget to wash my right hand. I figured, "Well, nothing touched it anyways, so there is no reason to wash it if it isn't dirty, right?" Wrong! My parents always asked me if I had washed both hands and if I said "no" and that it wasn't even dirty, they'd send me right back to the sink to wash both hands. If they saw me washing just one, they'd say, "Hey! Nika, wash both your hands, eh. It is a part of you. Do not neglect it; wash it too." They felt that using the excuse of it not being dirty wasn't the real reason, but rather that I didn't really like my arm at all. Over the years of constantly being told to wash both every time, it has become automatic to me to wash both my hands, all the time. Weird enough, when I shower, I obviously wash my right arm.

Only rarely do I forget, and right before I turn the tap off, while washing my hands at the sink, I hear a little voice in my head, like my parents', telling me to wash both and not to neglect my right hand. It's a really good thing, because I believe a couple years went by without me ever making that mistake again.

It was a great lesson learned about self-acceptance. They really disliked when I showed signs of self-hatred, and they did everything in their power to help me to see the beauty in my flaws and to accept myself as whole. Unfortunately, it was the environment and the ignorant people outside of my home that made me feel another way and that reversed the hard work my parents were putting in. It took many years of growth and building my self-confidence and self-image to see this for myself, although I am still in the process of bringing myself to that point of full self-acceptance.

Pushing carts & strollers with one hand — I hurt my wrist sometimes by pushing the cart with just my left hand, because my right wrist usually starts to hurt from pushing, and so I end up using only my left hand. Then, due to the heaviness of the cart, after a while my left wrist will begin to hurt as well. I just do it without complaining.

Washing my hair with one hand — In order to squeeze shampoo out of a bottle, I have to open the bottle upside down, hold it under my right arm, and push my arm against the wall to get it to start pouring out. Then there's the regular routine - I rub all of it in my hair until it lathers up then rinse it out. I repeat these steps twice then do the same for the conditioner, but just once. Whether I blow dry or towel dry, doing it with one hand the whole time and not being able to alternate makes my left arm fatigue easily. After my hair is finally dry, I add a bunch of hair products to keep my thick hair moisturized and healthy then throw on a hair bonnet or ask for someone to help me put it in a protective style – cornrows if I want to wear a wig or tie it up in a scarf until I'm ready to go somewhere.

Carefully standing on a bus or train —Just in case there is a hard stop and I find it hard to hold on, I ask someone for a seat. This is sometimes hard, and people give me a funny or rude look, not realizing I have a disability and that I could get hurt because I am only depending on one hand to keep me stable. There have been many times when a bus or train did a hard stop or a sharp turn while I wasn't holding on to something, because my left hand was full, and I tipped over. Most of the time, I've been able to stop myself, and the times when I couldn't, I really hurt myself by falling, bumping into someone else or a seat or pole in front of me. I'd honestly rather commute in the comfort of my own vehicle.

Falling — Ever since I was young, I have always been told, "When you fall, try to land on your bum or left side so you don't hurt your right arm, because you can't stick it out to break your fall. If you are falling forward, flex your stomach to absorb some of the blow, and cover your right arm with your left arm, and stick your chin up so your face doesn't hit the ground." In college, during the 2015 winter semester, I was with my friend from class and I slipped and fell hard on the black ice not too far from the door. I landed on the pavement on my left side to save my right arm, slightly injuring the side of my thigh, and I fell even harder on my left hand, injuring my wrist and thumb. My palm was scratched up, and the area around my thumb and index finger began to swell. I swore I had broken it, and it hurt like heck to move it around. I limped with my friend to the security office, because I needed to report the fall immediately. On my way there, I began to cry, not because of the pain, but because of the fact that I had injured my left hand. It's one of my biggest fears, because if I injure my left side then I may become truly dependent on someone to always help me.

I've always wondered what it would be like if something ever happened to my left side, since I use that arm to do everything, and that day that fear came to life. They took a look at my hand and asked me if I wanted to call an ambulance or if I wanted to transport myself to the hospital to get an X-ray. My father came to pick me up and take me to the hospital, and I got an

X-ray. Thank goodness, nothing was broken or fractured, just slightly sprained. I didn't have to wear a brace. I was told to minimize my activities, and rest it as much as I could. I mean, sure, it seems pretty easy to say "Just rest it", but it truly wasn't. From the moment I wake up and roll out of bed, everything I do requires me to use my left hand, starting with turning the knob on my bedroom door, which hurt a lot while I was recovering from the injury.

For two weeks I couldn't type or write. When I went to school I got a note-taker, which came in handy. My family also helped me to get little things done—my sister helped me get dressed, my brother did my chores (after two weeks, I faked it to get him to continue doing my chores without paying him). My dad prepped my food, and drove me to and from school so I wouldn't have to take the bus. Having my dad drive me to school was helpful because I couldn't hold on to anything if I had to stand on the bus. He also carried my things into the school for me. My professors, in partnership with the Centre for Students with Disabilities on campus, were very understanding and accommodating, which made the healing process easier and ensured that I didn't fall behind. Those two weeks were a major wake up call for me, because it made me realize that I really needed to be careful with my left arm and hand. Not just in terms of falling, but also in terms of everything I do—lifting heavy things, not massaging the bone joints and muscles, writing or typing excessively, or doing anything repetitively that puts strain on my hand and causes pain. The everyday things I do feel like I'm on autopilot, because I've been doing them my entire life, without even realizing how much I am hurting myself. It's only later once I start to feel the pain that I realize I need to minimize everything I do and ask for more help.

I wanted to do hair as well as my mother can, but I cannot. I wanted to open a hair salon and everything. Yes, of course, I could've had assistance, but I wanted to be able to braid, cornrow, flat iron, curl, perm, treat, and colour my clients' hair like any other hairdresser. I know they say, "Where there's a will, there's a way", but that just wasn't in the cards for me. Not that

I didn't learn or didn't know how, because I was eager to do it, it's just that I'm physically limited. I'm serious when I say that all I ever wanted to do was put my hair in a ponytail. That's it, a simple, quick, messy ponytail. I know how, I've seen an amazing YouTube video of how a young woman did it, but I tried then quickly realized I couldn't. When I realized my afro wouldn't wrap and hold in place against the wall like the young woman's pin-straight hair in the video, and for a brief moment, a wave of self-hatred came over me; just a brief moment. Then I decided to cut off all my hair—"the big chop."

Doing my own hair — I was mad most days when I woke up in the morning and stared at myself in the mirror, because I could not put my own hair up in a ponytail. I'd stand there for so long, staring until I got pissed off at the fact that I had a disability. "Why me?" I'd stand there and say. "This is so unfair!" I'd snap. I've actually banged my left fist on my dresser a few times, because I felt just so fed up. The task requires two hands, and my mother wasn't always around to help me put my hair in a simple ponytail. That took away my independence and depressed me. At times, I'd stare in the mirror wondering, "What am I going to do with this out-of-control hair of mine without my mom being around to help me?" Most of the time, I had no choice but to brush it down the best way I could and leave it out. I can't even braid my hair in two. I get the weaving concept, but I cannot do it without two hands. Same thing goes with putting my hair up in a ponytail; I know how to do it, but I just can't. I've tried many times, in many different ways, but I just cannot do it. Would you believe that I taught my little sister how to put her hair up in a ponytail? I knew the technique and told her how to do it. My best friend was at my home at the time and helped me by showing her the visuals and doing what I said to do alongside her.

My mom used to do all my "wicked" up-do hairstyles for me. Some of my friends would ask me to ask her if she could do their hair like that. She'd set a date and do it for them whenever she had the time. As she became busier at work and I reached high school, she found a hairstylist whom she paid to do my hair every once in a while. Whenever my hair wasn't done up, I'd wake up and attempt to tie my hair with a scarf. She'd do it for me, and then she taught me a way to do it myself with one hand. It did take me way longer, but I learned how to do it myself, and it was great, but only if my hair was corn-rowed back already to sit properly underneath. If my hair wasn't already braided, it would look super "poufy" when I tied the scarf myself. But, I would still have to go to school. In high school, they had a rule about wearing scarves and hats, unless it was for religious purposes. I understood, but at the same time I never cared, because my hair was very coarse and thick. Leaving it out all the time did not always look presentable but I'd take my scarf off if my hair wasn't too bad underneath.

In grade ten I really had it out with my principal one day for telling me to take off my hat or else she'd suspend me for a day. I was sent to the office by my teacher for refusing to take it off, even though I tried to explain why I had it on in the first place. My mom wasn't home that morning to help me put my hair up, so I just hauled on a knitted winter beanie to cover my hair all day instead of taking it off when I got to school. This was already embarrassing, because the class was hearing everything. Instead of understanding the situation, my teacher continued to call me out in front of my class, and I got pissed off, and it turned into a screaming match as he got up in my face. Then a hall monitor came to get me. I was cool with that hall monitor, so I blew off some steam on my way to the office, explaining what had happened. I got to the office, and the principal already had an attitude, sternly telling me to take off the scarf. I said "No" and tried to explain why, but she continued to tell me to take it off in front of everyone, including the other students who were there. I felt embarrassed and called her out on her ignorance.

I remember saying something along the lines of "You have pin-straight hair, and can wake up in the morning, just quickly brush your hair and go about your business and still look presentable. Can you put your hair in a ponytail? Of course you can. Now try with doing it with one hand, I bet you can't. I'd pay you if you could. Even if I attempted to brush it like you, my hair is a different and coarser texture than yours." She tried cutting me off, and I cut her back off, continuing with my rant. "But with my hair, getting out of bed and brushing it in a ponytail is impossible without having help from someone." At this point, I began crying and screaming at top of my lungs. "I already told you what happened this morning, but you didn't want to listen, I have a disability, and thanks for embarrassing me for trying to hold on to some sort of independence—" She had cut me off to tell me to sit and calm down. I revved up and then lost my composure entirely. "No! You're being ignorant, f**k off! Suspend me! I don't care, I'm going home!" I walked out of the school and mentally prepared myself to be expelled for what I had done. I went home and told my parents what I had done and why I was home so early. They understood my frustration, but felt I could've handled the situation in a better manner. I agreed, but at the same time I was fed up, and this woman had called me out on one of my major insecurities. My parents urged me to go to school the next day, and regardless of what I felt, I needed to respectfully apologize to my principal.

I went back to school the next day and did exactly that. A crazy, anxious feeling came over me as I sat there in the office at 8:30 a.m. before school started. I saw her walking around the office, looking very busy. I rolled my eyes while letting out a heavy sigh, then I opened the office door. She didn't notice me until I called out to her, and I thought she would have just suspended me for real, right then and there. She stopped in the midst of whatever she was doing, and before she could even respond I just kept apologizing for my disruptive and inappropriate behaviour. She kept staring back at me and motioned for me to follow her to her office. I proceeded into her office and grabbed a seat, still apologizing. At that point, I was pleading in hopes she wouldn't suspend me, or worse, expel me. I stopped to take a deep breath, and she held her hands together, looked down then looked up at me and told me she understood why and that she was very sorry for not being considerate, refusing to hear me out, and for not understanding. I couldn't believe she was apologizing to me. I just sat there, and she assured me that I was not being suspended and that I had permission to wear a hat or scarf whenever I needed to, due to my situation. I could see it in her face that she was giving a sincere apology as well. She told me she'd talk to that teacher that sent me down to the office. She also said that if another teacher, or even a hall monitor, questioned me because of what was on my head, or told me to take it off, to tell them I had permission from her, and if they had any other concerns they could speak to her about it. From that day forward, she was one of my favourites in the school, always laughing up with me and checking in on me, until she left when I reached grade eleven. Around that year, I found a few friends who could do hair, and I'd pay them to do my hair.

When I graduated and went to college, this wasn't an issue, ever. I felt more freedom, and wore scarves and hats like they were running out of style. I paid for my hair to get done once a month, because I really didn't want to wear my hair under a hat or scarf in a top knot all the time. I only did this when my hair started looking a bit trashy. My mom also helped with my hair in the mornings, to put it up and braid it, whenever she could. When my mother passed away before my second year of college, it became even harder to maintain my hair. I'd always have to pay to get it done once a month, or I'd call and ask my godmother, who didn't live too far away, to assist me in braiding my hair or putting it in a long ponytail up-do. My cousin, who lived three blocks up the street at the time, would often get up out of her sleep to come over and help me put my hair up. Even when I didn't ask for help, and she and our other best friend saw something that I may or may not need help with, they'd jump up and do it just like my family. Those girls are my sisters and I have been truly blessed to have a wonderful, loving, supportive family and good friends. I don't know what I'd do without them. I know they never, ever have an issue with helping me with my personal care, but I hate bothering them. They don't see it as a bother, of course, but I do feel that way sometimes when I know I have to ask for help.

The main reason why I cut off my hair was that I was fed up with always needing help. But another reason was that I was tired of not seeing my own natural hair. Since the age of ten, my hair has been "permed" or chemically relaxed, every few months, because it was so curly, coarse and thick. I went swimming quite often when I was younger, and the chlorine definitely damaged my hair. The ends kept thinning and splitting, and my hair always felt dry. On top of all this, putting gel in my hair to slick it back, as well as applying heat with a blow dryer or flat- or curling-iron added to the damage. Eventually, I got fed up. I was fed up with not being able to deal with my natural hair myself and with seeing so much of my hair fall out into a comb when I washed it. I wanted to see and feel my natural, unprocessed hair. When I used to perm my hair and a few weeks went by, I'd feel my natural coiled curls about an inch from my roots, but that wasn't enough for me. I wanted to see it. More of it.

On April 9, 2016, I decided that I wanted to cut off all my hair and go natural. That is when I began my hunt for a good natural hairstylist in Toronto. I found one and she did such an amazing job. She took her time to cut my hair carefully and evenly. I had never cut my hair before, so I was scared. In the past, the only thing I'd ever done was trim the ends after a perm, but to cut it right off was almost a culture shock for me. Since it was the first time anyone had cut off my hair, she felt honoured to do so. I was sad to see my hair go, but anxious to see my natural afro. I felt free and felt the cool summer breeze against the top of my head. The only thing is that I had become self-conscious about what others would think of my super-short hair.

I left the hairstylist's house and took a picture in the elevator on the way down. I walked outside and it was sunny with clear skies. I felt a sense of newness when the wind passed over my head; I actually felt it on my scalp, and it felt so good! I went from having hair a bit past my shoulders to being nearly bald. It took me a few weeks to get used to this new look and feel. I couldn't wait to start seeing the growth of my hair. As it began to grow, I looked at myself and began to fall in love with myself more and more, embracing my natural beauty. I loved it and I still do today. It's been two years now, and my natural hair is at a healthy couple of inches long; when some of the coils are pulled and stretched, the hair strand is about four inches from my scalp, which is wonderful growth. Continuing to keep up with a regular hair-care regimen will help my hair to continue to grow beautifully and healthily.

There are many ways that I can do things for myself, though sometimes I put myself at risk of getting hurt in the long run. That's because I'm still fighting to be as independent as possible and less dependent on others for my health and safety - like my mom wanted me to do. I'm learning to swallow my pride and ask for help, without feeling ashamed. Things like putting on a necklace, putting on earrings with a backing, tying a scarf, tying my shoes, or putting on gloves are difficult to do with one hand, though I always try to do them myself. I can explain how I do each one of these little things, but without a visual it's hard to imagine. I've seen the look people give me while turning their heads to the side, trying to fathom how I do some of the things I do.

Putting on a necklace or a watch requires assistance from someone else. I find this quite annoying. Same thing goes for earrings that have a backing. If the necklace has a big opening, I can just put it over my head. I won't say it's impossible to put on a watch by myself, because I've tried it recently by using my teeth and pushing against a wall, and after ten minutes of continuous attempts in desperation to get it done myself, I was finally able to get it. I did hurt my teeth a bit from the tugging and pulling, however. I showed my dad because I was so happy that I did it, although I struggled greatly, and I showed him how I did it. Of course, he was happy I had gotten it on my own, but he was more upset, and I saw his eyes begin to water, because he said it was unfair to me, and had things gone the way they were supposed to at birth, I wouldn't have to be doing this. He also told me that I needed to really stick to asking for help to keep from injuring myself. I know he is right, but I hate hearing it because I'm the perseverant type who strives to be independent. Hate is a very strong word, and I repeat, I hate it.

Sometimes I go to get my nails done at the salon, because when I use my mouth to hold the brush between my teeth to paint my left finger nails, it puts my health at risk. Not only am

I inhaling the fumes, but also sometimes the brush slips and drops on my bottom lip or chin, which is really gross. I've been going to the same salon for about four years, and sometimes when I go there, the ladies roll their eyes or become a bit rough when handling my hand, out of ignorance. I can read their body language and see that they are displeased when my right hand slips while they're working on my nails due to lack of control. It messes up the polish sometimes, and they have to start over or they sit there and hold my hand so it doesn't move, while my other hand dries. I usually sit there feeling ashamed, because other customers will sit and stare while sometimes two salon technicians work on my nails at the same time. I hate when they use toe-spacers to separate my fingers to keep them from smudging each other; I find it embarrassing.

There have been many times when I've overheard other people, even young women my age, laughing and whispering about me, and I'd roll my eyes. I have started blasting music through my earphones whenever I go there, so I don't have to hear their bullshit or hear the ladies working and complaining in their language. They'll tell me sometimes that I should be their last appointment of the day, around 8:30 p.m., because I require too much time and work, which interferes with their other appointments. Why can't they just be accommodative, instead of making it seem as if dealing with a client with a disability is a burden to their business? I've gone to other salons, but realized that they're worse in the way they treat me, and I just can't bother with it, so I just stick to the one I always go to and suck it up.

I love learning new recipes, but for the sake of safety, I require assistance when cooking and baking. I have always been determined to cook since I was twelve years old. I loved making sandwiches as well, especially tuna sandwiches. In order to cut the tuna can open, I needed either a can opener or I'd have to do it the old school way by using a knife. Knowing I'd get in major trouble for doing it the old school way, because we did not have a one-touch can opener, I'd have to sneak and do it. My way of doing it was extremely dangerous, but I just didn't want to ask for help. I was so hard-headed and determined, but as my mom used to say, "Who nuh hear must feel." I definitely felt it one day, and that's when I cut it out for good. I'd rinse the top of the can and the knife, and sometimes dry it with a paper towel. The day I got injured I hadn't dried the can or the knife, which left an extra-slippery surface. I'd rested my whole right hand over the can, leaving a little space so I could make the first cut. Just imagine the horror scene with my right hand on the can and me taking a knife and jabbing the can, just nearly missing my right hand. I didn't end up stabbing my hand, but I was holding the can at an opening while continuing to cut around it without a secured grip. The wet surface made the knife slip and cut my hand. I showed my parents, and they were furious with me. My mother was close to tears. They helped me get cleaned up, scolded me on kitchen safety and told me to ask for help when cutting something. Now, before I decide to cook or bake, I try to make sure someone is home to help me. If it involves boiling and draining water in a big pot that requires carrying both sides, then I'll avoid it, but if it's a small pot with a long handle, then I will take the risk.

My dad cooks and cleans most of the time, but I feel bad that I can't help sometimes because of the exhaustion pain in my muscles, especially in my left arm, both shoulders, neck, and back. However, sometimes I will push myself and straighten up my room, vacuum, wipe down upholstery and other small chores. I enjoy sweeping as well, but I can't sweep with two hands, so when I sweep with one hand, it puts a strain on my left forearm, left wrist, the left side of my neck, and left shoulder, causing pain later. After getting the dust swept up in a pile, I couldn't sweep the rest of the pile into a dustpan, so my father showed me how to use my foot to hold the dustpan in place while sweeping the mess into it. This works, but sometimes I'll completely miss the dustpan or accidently kick the dustpan or step on it, spilling out the contents. I love doing laundry, but my brother, sister, or my dad has to follow me and carry everything to the laundromat, while I carry the detergent bottles or an empty basket and load the money on the card at the machine. If it is a light load then I will hug the basket to my left side and carry it. I love to fold clean clothes, it takes me a while longer, but I love to do it with help as well. There are times when I say, "Forget it, let me do this myself," and make multiple trips to the laundromat without asking for help. I'd grab the laundry card and load it up downstairs, then come back upstairs to take the basket of clothes, and drag it on the floor to the laundry, trying not to lift it up.

CHAPTER 5

Bullies Made Me Hate Myself

Mom and Dad taught me smart comebacks that would work, without me having to swear. For example, if someone called me a "fat, ugly, retarded bitch," I would say, "I know you are, but what am I?" And I'd repeatedly say it until they got annoyed and walked away. Because of the way my arm is turned, some kids would make fun of me by mocking how it is and laughing at it, which angered me. I continued to be a smart-mouth without swearing, but many times that alone wouldn't work, so I began cursing back at them. They'd run and tell the teacher or the principal, and guess who got in trouble for swearing? Me. Even when they did get in trouble, I'd still get in trouble too. I didn't really have friends to take my side and defend me. Many times, the ones who were two-faced would ride the bandwagon when it was convenient for them not to be bullied or not to get in trouble at school. This left me to defend myself alone in times of trouble, meaning it was my word against the rest of them. The same thing happened when I got into physical fights. Thankfully, my last fight was in grade eight, but it was against two girls. The ability to physically defend myself was all in my legs and very strong left arm. I used my left to punch, slap, grapple, and swing the bully around. When needed, I'd swing my right arm to hit them with my wrist. Of course, at that point I was also hurting myself, but I did whatever I could to get them to back off. My parents also taught me how to block and use my legs and left arm to fight and defend myself to the best of my ability.

Another defense mechanism was to always reassure myself

that I am a very beautiful and intelligent girl, to always wear a smile on my face, and to never let anyone ruin my day. Mom used to write affirmations hidden in places like my school books, yearbooks, reading books, and lunch box, all throughout my elementary, middle, and high school years to surprise me and make my day. I read them then smiled and laughed because, in a hilarious way, she made sure to remind me of how beautiful, smart, and strong I am. I loved that so much that I started doing that for my younger sister, and I will definitely be doing the same thing for my children when the time comes.

Some teachers graded me based on my physical ability to do things, rather than on my effort to try. An example of this was me getting a failing grade for not being able to shoot the basketball in gym class the "correct" way, instead of giving me a passing grade for getting the ball in the hoop my way and at least for trying.

I faced a lot of emotional distress in elementary school. My parents told me it was mostly because the children never really understood my disability. No one knew what brachial plexus injury was, not even adults, so I got bullied a lot for it. I used to get teased about my arm's condition and my right shoulder being higher than my left. They would put up their hands to their chest, tap against their chest, and call me "retarded, ugly, and stupid." I remember being emotionally, socially, physically, and spiritually bullied for my condition. I remember always having to explain my condition to people; they were also afraid to ask me because they thought they would offend me. I never understood why they were afraid though, because I loved educating others about my disability. Some people would even tell me, after I told them about my disability, that they were actually scared to ask me.

I was always embarrassed by my right arm and not being able to do things like other kids, so I would hide my right arm in a sweater pocket, or hide it with a bag or book. Getting bullied on a daily basis made me scared to go back and face the bullies the next day, so I'd often make excuses to stay home. However, my parents never bought it. At school I'd make up a reason to see the school nurse or say I wasn't feeling well so I could have someone come to sign me out and take me home.

I was always isolated from social groups on the playground, so I would play by myself. I remember tying a skipping rope to a pole or tree on some days and skipping by myself, since I couldn't hold the other side with my right arm. It was so bad that my mom had to teach me different ways to have fun by myself. As I got older, she told me having to do that saddened her. I don't remember the name of the game, but my mom once put a tennis ball in a pair of panty hose that she had cut off, and she told me to stand with my back against a wall at recess and swing the ball to hit the wall over my head, over my shoulders, across my arms, and between my legs. This game was super-fun to me. Watching me play, the same damn bullies made fun of me at first, but a few days later they were begging me to try it. I couldn't wait to run home that very day and tell my parents, laughing at how they actually wanted to play with me. And, literally, the next day after letting them play, they were back to isolating and bullying me.

I usually sat by myself during recess and lunch, watching other children play, or I'd hide in a corner and cry because no one would play with me. I didn't really have any friends to eat lunch with, so I would sit alone and not socialize with anyone. I'd sometimes eat in the principal's office and sit there and talk with her. If she was busy, I would sit outside in the main office and eat there. I refused to go outside after I ate sometimes, and preferred to sit at the little round table they had in the main office and spend the rest of the lunch recess drawing or something like that. I remember spending many of my recesses sitting on a little hill near the playground, and I'd watch kids run pass me and look at them, anxiously waiting for an invite to play, but more often than not, I never got one. I remember attempting to make amends with the bullies by going up to them and just standing by them to see if they'd let me play with them. But when I stood close to the group, they'd walk away from me, giving a clear signal that they didn't want to play with me. Since waiting and approaching became a "no go," I began talking to teachers sometimes, but after a while it got embarrassing, because the other kids caught on when they saw me standing by the teacher for the whole recess, and made fun of me even more for trying to make friends with the teacher after being isolated by them. In grade one, I was playing with another student in my class outside in the snow, when a little boy threw a snowball in my direction and at the very last second shouted, "Heads up!" I looked up and the snowball hit me right in my mouth, splitting my top lip and also knocking out my two top front teeth, which I spat right into my hands and took to the office. The Tooth Fairy definitely did me up nicely with the green money—twenty dollars—which felt like a thousand dollars to me back then. The principal was going to give him an office suspension for rough playing outside, but I defended him and said it was an accident so he wouldn't get into trouble.

I had two best friends who used to protect me against bullies by defending me when they were around and played with me when no one else would. They moved away when we were in grades two and three. They never judged me or turned their backs on me when two-faced friends did. I never ever had to bribe them to be my friend. Every time I made a friend after a few days or weeks, I'd lose them to the clan of my main bullies. I got in big trouble with one of them one day for staying late after school until 4:00 p.m. (half-an-hour after the school bell rang). We were supposed to go home straight after school but instead she and I were caught playing in the snow after everyone had dispersed from the school property and our parents couldn't find us. We both got in big trouble and we weren't trusted to come home straight after school by ourselves for a while, even though our building was right behind the school.

I used to get bullied on Facebook in grade six by some rude kids in my classes. Mom had my password, but I never told her about it, she discovered it on her own. She got furious and printed out the messages for the principal to see. The girls were all suspended.

When I complained about the bullying to my teachers or the principal sometimes, they wouldn't do much. There were many times when they'd drag out their "investigations", so I'd retaliate to the bullying, which in most cases got me consequences. I'd hit back, and if they called me names like "fat," I'd say something like "Under your mother" or "Your face." Those kids would gang up and tell the principal some lie to either get me in trouble or prove they never did anything to me first for me to retaliate. Since I never had anyone to back me up, those kids who were friends of my bullies became "witnesses" to the principal. It wasn't fair. If they found that the kid actually did something to me, and I retaliated, we would both get the same punishment. It would stop them from bothering me, maybe for that day, but things would go right back to normal the next day.

Growing up, I really enjoyed being a part of multicultural show nights, craft nights, movie nights, book fairs, and other activities, because I found all of these to be a lot of fun. They were inclusive, and I loved feeling a sense of belonging. I also thought gym class was really fun because of the activities the teacher had planned for the whole class. But when it came to anything that had to do with teaming up with other classmates, I dreaded it, especially if it was up to the class to find their own partners or teammates. I was always the last choice for team captains during gym class, or the teacher would place me by default in a group, but since no one chose me. They didn't choose me because they thought I would cause them to lose the games since I was physically limited from doing certain activities, like catching or throwing a ball. Sometimes the meanest of kids would make a huge scene in front of everyone about why they never wanted me and the teacher would put them in their place, of course. When the teacher forced them to keep me on their team I felt so bad that I wanted to leave the class, because I could see it on their faces that they weren't pleased with me being on their team. I wouldn't take part in gym class some days; I would ask to use the bathroom and not return, because I would cry and hide somewhere. I thought everything required two hands, like push-ups and carrying things or shooting a basketball. Whenever I couldn't do something I would be made fun of by the entire class. I eventually stopped trying.

No one ever wanted me in their group for class activities either, so I found myself either working alone or embarrassed because I had to work with the teacher as a partner, then I would get teased for it. I remember doing class projects by myself the majority of the time. In earlier years, I wasn't afraid to go around the class and ask people if I could be in their group, even though I was usually rejected. I never knew why I was rejected because I had never done anything to anyone. Sometimes I would still try and say the group needed four people if I saw a group of three and I'd ask to be the fourth in their group; they'd still say "no" to me. Teachers would force a group to accept me but I still wasn't welcomed. The thing was, I would put in more work than those other students. My parents made sure I could prove to the teacher that I was not hindering the group from excelling at any project. I remember my mother complaining to the teacher that my doing most of the work was unfair. I'd get the group an A+, but their individual efforts weren't equally deserving of an A+, so the teacher would have to just give me the A+ and then mark the others individually. I really didn't care, because they never wanted me in their group in the first place, proving I was better off on my own. I took on that attitude as the school years went by. Instead of begging to be in a group, I would just take on the whole project by myself. However, I got a lot of help at home from my parents. They never did the work for me, because they wanted me to produce my own work and prove my honesty, but they'd help me put it together. They'd also fight for extensions for me, since I was doing the projects on my own.

There was one girl, Kayla, that I hated a lot. She tormented me on a daily basis. For most of my bullying experiences, she was the root of the problem, a major instigator. There was a group of about five kids who always bothered me along with her, but she was the worst one in the group. She turned the one or two friends I had in elementary school against me. Whenever a new student came to the school, I'd make friends with them quickly, but after a while, when they got to know Kayla too, she'd ruin the friendship for me by telling them that I got bullied, or she'd make fun of the fact that I was "fat" and called me "retarded,". One day in grade two, I got into a huge fight with Kayla at recess. I repeatedly slammed her into the wall of the school when I had had enough of her shenanigans. She had yanked my hood, and when I turned around and saw that it was her, I lost it. I took my left hand and grabbed her by the coat collar, and yelled, "Stop both-e-ring me-e-e-e!" She hit the wall with every syllable and I stepped on her foot. Everyone ran to Kayla's rescue, but they could not see the countless provocations that led up to me doing that. I put up with so much and I felt she deserved every hit. I remember letting go and when I went in for a swing, a yard-duty teacher grabbed my arm and began dragging me to the office. Well, of course, I was the bad student, because Wynnikka was the bully that went around beating kids up for no reason, right? Wrong. Kayla backed off for a while but that fight obviously wasn't enough to keep her off me for long. In grade 4, she and her bully clan followed behind me one day after school. I took my time getting home, so there were fewer parents and witnesses around to see what happened. She called out to me, and I was near my building, so I kept my head straight. When she realized that I hadn't responded to her, she ran up and yanked my backpack off my back, hurting my right shoulder and arm in the process.

That backpack was my favourite backpack ever. It was a lilac Bratz Doll backpack with sparkles, three zip compartments, and all the characters on the front. I told her to give it back, and her little minions blocked me and began laughing at me. She saw a pile of dog poop that was quite fresh and threw my bag in it, which angered me. She then stomped all over it, along with the other kids. I wanted to pick it up but remembered there was dog poop on it, so I began to cry. Just when I thought they were through, one of them grabbed it by the handle and threw it over a sign post so I couldn't reach it. I didn't know how to react other than to cry and go home. I walked into my house and when my dad saw me crying hysterically, he became angry and asked what happened. He ran outside, forgetting he was in his boxers, to see who it was and to get my bag. As I followed him, I told him that I didn't want the bag anymore. I was also embarrassed about my father being seen by a few people in his boxers and running shoes. My parents bought me the exact same backpack again, with fresh supplies and everything, but the bullying didn't end there.

At school, I always hid in the bathroom during recess. Some teachers caught on and wouldn't let me inside or they'd come to find me because they didn't see me leave the washroom to go back outside. I only hid because I was being bullied. I did it to avoid crossing paths with the bullies who would torment me because of my arm. The teachers didn't care. They'd say, "If you don't stop doing this, Wynnikka, I will report your behaviour to your teacher and the office. So please go outside and stop with these excuses." I'd say to myself, "Oh, I'm sorry for trying to find a way to avoid bullying, since no one is really doing much about it anyway."

I believe I got bullied so much because my peers were ignorant about my disability and didn't understand. They also saw me as an easy target. I have a huge heart. I'm too kind, I'm too generous, and I am easily forgiving. I guess no one taught them any better, so I cannot blame them entirely for their behaviour. They were just children.

My mother would call the school trustee and superintendent to do their investigations, since the school wasn't doing much about the bullying that I went through daily. Whenever this happened, and they sent lengthy emails to the school, the school would react fast in getting those kids dealt with when they bothered me. If authorities higher than the school had to be contacted, then the matter was serious, and they took it very seriously. Due to being bullied, I bounced around and went to four different elementary schools up until grade six. However, each new school was just as bad as the previous one. The worst one was my home school, because when I went outside to the park outside of school hours, those same kids came and bullied me in the park. It didn't stop me from playing outside though. Sometimes I'd bribe them by sharing popsicles or candy in the summer so they'd leave me alone at the park, but it wouldn't work for more than about a day.

Kids at school mocked the way I clapped with one hand. During assemblies, we would sit down with our classes, and when we were clapping, I noticed that I couldn't clap like everyone else. So I would put my right hand in my lap and would use my left hand to tap my right hand to make the same clapping noise. I didn't have a problem with it, until some kids noticed and started to mock me. They called me retarded and deformed and copied the way I clapped to make fun of me. I got bullied so much one day at the park that I forgot about my baby sister and left her behind; they followed me. When I passed the gate of the school, I pushed past them and ran back for her.

I literally went home every day with another bullying story, and I would sometimes cry myself to sleep out of fear of what I would face the next day. After school, I would come home and take out my anger on my siblings by being mean or bossy and ignoring them. Sometimes I would pass mirrors and avoid looking at myself because I believed I was as ugly as the bullies continuously told me I was, although my parents and close family members tried to convince me of the opposite. Up until I was in grade twelve, I avoided looking at myself in the mirror. I couldn't look myself in the eye because, deep down, I felt bad about myself.

Mommy had a miscarriage after my younger sister was born. I used to think it was my fault. I remember a few days before she lost him she had stormed over to the school to confront my grade six teacher for making fun of me and embarrassing me in front of the whole class for not having any friends or project partners to work with in the class. I had gone home crying at lunchtime and Mommy handed me a garbage bag before we left the house and told me to pack my stuff from my desk. After that day, I switched schools for good and went to a junior public school that went up to grade six. After I graduated, I went to middle school for two years then to high school. I never moved schools again unless I graduated, which was excellent.

When I was graduating from junior public school in grade six, I didn't have many friends. As a matter of fact, I believe I only had one friend. There was a rehearsal the day before graduation, and we were called up one by one. We received a paper, practiced how to do the exchange and handshake, then walked off the stage and returned to our seats. I remember everyone being called up and everyone clapping each time. When I was getting ready to go up, because my name had been called, a girl I really disliked turned to a few kids around her and told them to tell everyone else not to clap for me. I honestly felt that at least some of the kids wouldn't have listened to her and would have still clapped, but it was dead silence when I got up there. After I heard just the teacher clapping, it really hit me hard, and as I was walking off the stage to return to my seat, I began to cry. I walked out of the gymnasium and went to the washroom. When I came back, the teacher was talking to the class about what they had done including the girl who started it all. I remember the girl leaving to go to the office. That incident crushed me so much but, of course, at graduation my parents screamed and clapped as I was going up to accept my diploma. Other parents and teachers were clapping for me as well, so I really didn't care about those mean kids who sat there and didn't clap for me.

During the summer before I went to middle school—when I was around twelve years old—I reached a point where I couldn't take the bullying anymore and grabbed anything sharp I could find and cut my right arm with it. I remember taking a plastic hanger, cracking it in half, and using the sharp end to cut my right arm a couple of times. Some of the scars are still visible. My mother died without ever knowing that I had cut myself. I regret not having that conversation with her. She saw the marks covered by Band-Aids that I had put on myself and she became furious. When I was younger, my parents always called me "extra" for wanting a Band-Aid for every little cut I got. Of course, I lied to her saying I had fallen off my bike on the paved hill at the park, then she looked at me funny and told my father, who also got furious. They took my word for it, since I'd never shown any other signs of self-harm at the time. I reached a point where I really hated how my right arm caused me to not have any friends and caused me to get bullied every day, no matter what school I went to. I could never run away from it. But I failed to see that it wasn't me or the disability I have that was the issue, it was the ignorance of the other kids and their lack of compassion for others.

Bullies would tell me around the age of twelve that I would never have a boyfriend and that no one would ever like me because I was ugly, that I was fat and had a weird, looking arm. This occurred so often, both at school and at the park after school, that it made me hate myself even more. At that age, everyone began crushing on each other, and, of course, I had crushes on boys my age too. But no one ever crushed on me, ever (not that I knew of), and the bullies always made sure to tell me why. They told me things like I would embarrass my boyfriend, and that he would break up with me in less than a week, so I began to internalize all the things they said about me.

There were a few older people who began to watch out for me and defend me whenever they witnessed the bullying. Unfortunately, sometimes when kids would bully me they would bully my brother as well. I didn't say much at first, because I was scared they'd keep bullying me, so it's almost as if I let them bully my little brother so they wouldn't bully me. But then I stopped ignoring it, because I wasn't being a good big sister. He used to try and beat the kids up when I took him to the park, and they'd try to bully me like when I was younger. Our mom gave us her cell phone to call her just in case anything ever happened. Sometimes our father would stand at the back door of our building, facing the park, to observe what was happening with us outside, and if he noticed an issue, he'd come get us or sit there so we could play without being bothered. Our parents also had their friends and neighbours on higher floors look out at the park sometimes to see if there was anything going on, so they could attend to it faster.

No matter what these kids did to me, no matter how much they bullied, taunted, humiliated or isolated me, I was always willing to be their friend. I was never rude to them. There were rare times when I got the strength, more often as I grew older, to face them and challenge them back, but I was a major pushover and was easily forgiving of others, to the point where they'd take advantage of me. I have forgiven them now. I still see them today, and as grown as we are now, I hold my head up high and say, "Hi." I will not allow what they did to me to turn me into a bitter person. They are the ones who have to live with the shame and guilt every time they see me now, so I couldn't care less about holding on to it. I killed them with kindness, because that was what I was taught to do. Of everything I tried, kindness was the only thing that worked.

Mommy and I would always reflect on all the bullying, isolation, and taunting I went through during elementary school, and one day during our conversation she began to cry. I hadn't been bullied in years, so I was shocked to see her still crying so much about it. I looked at her and said, "Mom, look at me, I overcame the bullying. I've made it further in life than my bullies at this age. I'm graduating college next year, and I'm about to start my summer job. Having them bully me like that only made me a stronger person today."

She then replied, while wiping her tears away, "Don't you give them credit for what your father and I, your loving siblings, other family members, friends, teachers, mentors, and coworkers have shaped you to become."

All I could do at that point was smile and hug her. I could still see the pain she was going through remembering what those harsh kids did to me throughout my elementary school years. Not only were the students terrible, but some teachers were as well. After my mom passed away, I logged into her email account and found lengthy emails that were written to the District School Board trustees and superintendents in desperation trying to get help with my bullying situations at school because the teachers and principals weren't doing anything much to stop it. I couldn't remember some of the content of the emails about things that happened to me during elementary school, but my parents remembered very clearly, and it still bothered them years later.

One day when we drove up to my sister's elementary school to drop her off, Mommy pointed out a little girl who looked like she had the same disability I had, except in both of her arms. She always walked with her same friend who helped her with everything. They looked like they were in grade five or so. Mom told me she had walked up to the little girl a few days earlier, before the morning bell. She asked to give her a big hug and told her that she had a daughter who was like her. She then told her that she could do whatever she put her mind to. She cried as she walked back to the car, because the little girl reminded her of how I looked when I was younger—same skin tone, same beautiful face, same chubbiness, and same happy-go-lucky attitude.

I saw her one day, and she was holding a basketball up with both her arms while walking with her friend. I walked my sister into the school, then stopped the little girl and her friend and reminded her of my mom. She said she remembered, and I became teary-eyed, because she definitely did look a bit like me. I knelt to her level, smiled, and asked to give her a big hug. I told her how beautiful she was and that she could do anything she wanted. I told her what grade I was in and how proud I was of her. I also told her not to let anyone bully her for having a disability, because she had a very bright future and she would inspire many one day. I felt I had to in the moment, but afterwards I realized how weird it must have looked for me to walk up to someone else's child like that and speak to them without permission from their parents or an authority figure at the school. But I felt it was important for me to say it.

Just like the time I saw a teenage girl at the bus stop near my old high school, who had a skin condition called Vitiligo. I had an urgency to remind her how beautiful she was. At first, I hesitated, because I didn't want to come off as creepy, but right before the bus arrived, I forced myself to do it. I told her how beautiful she was and not to let anyone bully her or ruin her day, because she had a bright future ahead of her. She thought, because I was looking at her, that I was judging her, but then when I was done saying what I had to say, she said, "Oh my gosh! No one has ever randomly said that to me, and it's my biggest insecurity. Thank you, I really appreciate that." She opened her arms for a hug, and I gave her a big hug. Why do I do things like this? I guess it's that big sister or motherly instinct to say it just in case they had never heard it before. It was her biggest insecurity and I positively reminded her to embrace her beauty.

The bullies ruined my confidence and my self-esteem completely during elementary school, all because of my disability. And the more I got bullied, the more I gained weight, which gave them another reason to make fun of me with fat jokes every day. I'd come home to try and eat it all away. I was eating when I wasn't hungry—cookies, ice cream, chocolate, cereal and milk, anything that tasted good and satisfied my cravings for acceptance. I stopped talking to my parents about who bullied me, because whenever I told them, they'd storm outside and approach the bully, demanding that they bring their parent or guardian outside so they could have a word with them about their child's unacceptable behaviour towards me. If the bullying incident was bad enough to send me home crying, they'd go outside, I'd point out the kid, and they'd curse the kid out until he or she cried. If, and when, their parents came to our door, some were apologetic and felt their child deserved that for bullying me, others challenged my mom and got the lecture and back-home Caribbean tell-off of their life, which sent them home in silence. Of course, that might not have been the right thing to do, but if talking to the parent wasn't enough and your child began to show signs of self-hate and negative self-talk, what would you have done after months of trying many different solutions that failed? I stopped talking to my parents about these incidents, because these same kids began to terrorize me for being a tattletale. Eventually, I just kept everything in. I stopped telling authorities at school and stopped telling my parents, because the day after one kid got in trouble, others would find out and call me a snitch. No one liked snitches, so those who were my friends on-and-off stopped talking to me because I was starting to become a snitch. To my parents, it just seemed as if the bullying was fading. I still reported some serious incidents, but I mostly began to eat my problems away and packing on the pounds. As I got older, by grade seven and eight in middle school, I barely got bullied. Although there were still a few bullies, I made a few friends at my new school with a new set of kids who didn't know me. It was such a positive culture for me that I had to ask my parents why no one was making fun of me. I'd become so immune to being bullied that I was just waiting for it to happen.

CHAPTER 6

Middle School Life Crisis

I was never the type to get attention from guys at all. As a matter of fact, my friends and I weren't the popular types when we got to high school, and I definitely wasn't before then. I was conditioned to believe that no guy would like or accept me for who I am externally. I couldn't find anything wrong with myself internally; I'm full of love, care, honesty, acceptance of others, trustworthiness, perseverance, and resilience. However, I believed everything externally was wrong with me, too wrong for me to be noticed by any guy I had a crush on. I could hear the words, "No one will ever date you, because of your arm and your weight," in my head. Of course, dating shouldn't have been on my mind at that time, but it's normal to begin wondering about it at that age, since everyone started having little crushes around that time. This mentality of self-hatred stuck with me for years, because the bullying had shut my self-esteem down. I never dated anyone in high school. I wasn't one of the prettiest ones, but I envied them all.

There was this one cute boy whom I always had a crush on growing up, on and off since my first day of kindergarten. He said his name and, because it sounded very similar to my brother's, I developed the biggest crush on him. When we were in the same class again in grade two, I remember handing him my eighth birthday party invitation, and he tore it up into pieces in front of everybody. I was so heartbroken, because I just wanted him there so I could cut the cake with him. My other mini-crush, who was also my friend, came and I cut the cake with him instead. There was a girl in my grade two class whom I hated very much, but he had a crush on her, and everyone knew it. When we were standing at our cubbies one afternoon, getting ready to go home, she started bothering me for no reason and pulled my backpack, so I slapped her. That boy came out of nowhere and fly kicked me hard in my stomach and told me to leave her alone. The teacher didn't see what happened, so I grabbed my things and ran outside to meet my dad. He saw me crying and became furious. He walked around the school yard to find the boy and his mother and yelled at him to leave me alone and to never put his hands or feet on a girl ever again. I stopped liking him for a few years after that. I actually hated his guts, until I was in grade six and he became nicer to me again.

By this age, it seemed as if whenever anyone had a crush on somebody, or was semi-dating them, the whole school and block knew, and not only did they know, but they were also heavily involved in the little puppy-love business, as if they were in it with them. Eventually, everyone found out I had a crush on him, because I told one two-faced friend my secret, and she went around and told everyone, including him. One boy, whom I thought was my friend, told me to my face that no guy our age in the area whom I liked would ever like me, because my arm was retarded and because I was fat and ugly. That tore me up inside, and I felt that the boy I liked wouldn't like me back for those same reasons. One day, a group of us were over at the basketball court near our school, and he was there. I was with my sister and brother and one of my so-called friends. We walked near the court and saw my crush standing there, playing basketball with his friends, and he took one last shot and missed, so everyone began laughing at him. He was laughing too, but you could tell he was embarrassed. He immediately walked over to me and asked me out. I had to stand there for a second to think if this dude was really talking to me or if I was sleeping. I came back to my senses fast and said, "Yes," as if he had proposed marriage to me. Looking back, it had to be the funniest and sweetest moment. We walked around together for a few minutes with all these kids following behind and asking me questions, such as if I was finally happy that a cute guy I liked asked me out. I calmly said, "Yeah, I guess," but on the inside I was screaming "Yes!" Soon it was time for me to take my siblings home, and I felt like the happiest girl in the world.

The next morning, it had to be a weekend morning because it was late morning and I was eating breakfast and watching cartoons when there was a knock at the door. I looked through the peephole and saw that it was him, so I stepped into the hallway, closing the front door behind me. I was just in my socks and pajamas. I was smiling and giddy, and then he said, "I need to tell you something, Wynnikka. We are over, what happened yesterday was a dare. Someone dared me as you were coming over from the park to the court to take a shot, and if I missed, I had to ask you out then break up with you the next day. I know you like me, but this was all fake, sorry. And I can't tell you who dared me to do it. Gotta go..." And that was it for me. After that day, I never told a guy I had a crush on him, until after high school. His younger brother, whom I was friends with, as well as my same so-called friend came to my front door a few hours later to tell me what I already knew. I was just really grumpy for the rest of the day, and cried in my room. I got quiet for a really long time. It was the talk of the school for a few days, maybe even for a few weeks, and I just wanted to disappear. I never started hiding my arm until I was in grade six.

"Guys don't want a girl like me. My arm is ugly, so they will be embarrassed and disgusted by me. And I'm fat," I told myself. I started eating more and packing on the pounds for comfort. I was eating and eating, whatever tasted good, way past the point of being full. I swallowed the shame and guilt, and it definitely showed later on.

I was always trying my hardest to prove myself academically, so that I wouldn't be judged by my disability. To be honest, it wasn't like that all the time, but I'd make the effort. And whenever I did, I went above and beyond, got extra help, and made sure my academics were on point, so that whenever people looked at me and dared to judge me based on my disability, I could find comfort in the fact that I was intelligent and educated, and no one could take it away from me.

My grade seven teacher rode his bike to and from school every day, as long as there wasn't any snow on the ground. I told him that I thought it was really cool, and he created a bike program where we learned about how to maintain our bikes, plan routes, and, most importantly, safety. I attended the program after school every week. One day, he took the group on a trip to ride our bikes and practice the safety techniques he had taught us. Just like drivers, cyclists must communicate when sharing the road, but instead of using indicators and other signals, we use our hands. While cycling with the group, I grew really frustrated, because I was already riding my bike with one hand, so I couldn't take my other hand up to signal left, right, or stop. Because I was with the group, and everyone was doing the same signal, it wasn't really a big deal, but what if I was by myself? I did ride my bike to and from school, but I never had to do a signal. Apart from that incident, I still enjoyed the program and continued to go.

It was the last day before Christmas break, and everyone was having a pretty relaxed last day of school. It was my eighth grade year, and I had kept from fighting bullies for many years through self-control. I remember vividly that it was music class, and everyone was assigned work that they had to complete or they couldn't leave for lunch. This teacher was one of my favourite teachers in the school at the time, aside from my grade seven teacher who happened to still be at the school. I had finished my work first, and it was ten minutes before the first lunch bell rang. The teacher said, "Okay, Wynnikka, since you were done first, go ahead and stand by the door and collect everyone's work as they leave. If it isn't complete, send them to me; they are not allowed to leave."

One particular girl, whom I despised, and her friend walked up to me and said, "Move."

I told them I wouldn't move until they showed me their work. At this point, I could've called on the teacher, but she was dealing with a line-up of students who hadn't completed their work.

The girl then said, "Move, you fat bitch."

I said, "I can show you where to find the fat bitch."

The first girl then shouldered me and pushed me out of her way, so I dragged her back by her shirt, and she spun around. I remember letting her go, then shoving her into the set of lockers behind her. We were tussling for a bit, and we both ended up on the floor. I had her by her hair and kicked her in her stomach before the teacher ran outside and broke it up. I was walking down the hallway yelling at her to try me again, and her friend turned around and threw her binder at me, telling me to shut the fuck up. I had had enough of being bullied. I picked up her binder, which had missed me by a metre or so, and tossed it back, hitting her shoulder, then I ran to punch and kick her. I was feeding her punches one after the other. I felt maybe one punch to my face, but not until after we were brought down to the office. Teachers came running out of their classes, and I kid you not, it took two teachers and my best friend in the school at the time to get me off of her. I was so outraged. My parents were called, and Dad came to get me in a snow storm. Yes, one thing I truly disliked every winter was that no matter how badly it was snowing, schools were always open. Buses got cancelled, but the schools remained open. Minus 25 degrees celsius with wind chill, 30 centimeters of snow, rain, sleet and black ice? No problem! We had no snow days ever, unless parents and guardians made the choice to keep their children at home.

Pictures were taken of the right side of my face, where there was a huge, deep scratch that was caused by the first girl whom I fought. I remember mom saying to my principal "I don't like how that damn girl has my daughter's DNA under her fingernails!"

It makes me laugh because it sounds really gross. Because they had started with me first, I was suspended for just the remainder of that day and the first day back to school after the holiday break. As for the girls, I remember them being gone for almost an entire school week. My mom also happened to get it off my student record a few months later, after speaking to the school superintendent, which was great for me. The funny thing was that all my school life, I never got suspended, until I had had enough of being bullied and finally retaliated, blowing the lid, letting out some serious steam.

I remember lying to the bullies for attention that year, saying I had had sex, had gotten pregnant and had gotten an abortion, in hopes that they'd feel bad and stop bullying me. Desperate times call for desperate measures so I thought of the worst thing to lie about. I told the bullies first, but the only reason why I told my best friend, Jae, outside the neighbourhood was because I feared that if I didn't tell her soon after telling them, they'd try to get her to not be my friend because of it when they saw her visiting me. I had given them a fake name for the boy I allegedly had sex with, and they started searching for this mysterious ninth grader boy on Facebook. When they weren't successful, that's when I began to worry. The lie dragged out for a while and most kids who found out began to believe me as I kept my word. Eventually everyone forgot and just left me alone. I was so embarrassed and ashamed of the fact that I had stooped that low at thirteen years old to hide the truth from her for years and then forgot about it. After grade twelve, I remembered it all over again in vivid detail, and felt that I really shouldn't hide such a silly lie anymore, so I revealed it to her. Believe it or not, I was quite anxious to mention it to her, but when I told her, she laughed because she couldn't believe I thought she would have stopped being my friend then, when she knew they were the ones bullying me. She also understood why I went to the extreme in an attempt to have them stop.

For my grade eight graduation, my parents got me a limo. I remember a month before graduation mom created a waiver form for me to hand to the five other students I wanted in my limo for their parent or guardian to sign. I had my very best friends come, and I had convinced my crush to come to dinner with us also. Before our graduation, there was this popular girl I didn't like that went around the school telling everyone she was getting a limo too, and charging them $5.00. Of course, because she was popular, everyone else wanted to go in her limo, but I had five solid friends, including the guy I had a crush on at the time, who signed the form and got them back to me so I could confirm with my mom. She wasn't charging my friends anything, not even for dinner.

On graduation day, everyone was inside the school, when a friend ran up to me and said, "I think your limo is outside, and it looks like a truck!" I went outside and saw this crisp snow-white, SUV limo, and I turned to look at my parents like they had lost their minds. Everyone crowded around the limo, waiting to hear if it was really mine, and so it was, so they had to back off and let my five other friends through. It was a graduation I'll never forget, because in that same year my sister had graduated from kindergarten so we were both celebrating. I stood there laughing, because everyone who chose the popular girl's limo was wondering where the limo was and wanted their $5.00 back. It turned out that the girl made about $100 off those kids, and didn't even have a limo booked to begin with. They were left there having to go home with their parents and guardians. I don't even know if those kids got their money back. Oh well, they should've stuck with the not-so-cool girl, Wynnikka.

My crush at the time took pictures handing me a bouquet of roses, and it was the cutest thing ever. It was kind of slimy because his little "girlfriend" was standing behind him with her parents, seeing everything. I didn't really like her anyway, so I couldn't have cared less. I strengthened my confidence by standing up to bullies and not taking their nonsense. And by the time I got to high school, I met more people who became my friends and were very supportive of me.

I was put in many programs outside of school, such as Sunday school, after school programs in the area, and girl guides. I played soccer on and off, here and there, but never for leagues. I was always in a camp as well, every summer, but because it was within our area, and it was with the same kids who would bully me, I couldn't dodge the bullying. My parents would get so mad that they would pull me out of the program and put me in camps that were outside of our area, but they didn't want to teach me to run away from my issues or my bullies. It did become too much sometimes, so they had to do what was best for me. I enjoyed the programs and all the activities they had to offer. These programs boosted my self-esteem by providing a strong sense of belonging and achievement. These programs also allowed me to feel comfortable, as they didn't tolerate bullying at all. In fact, they were on top of their game when it came to tackling bullying.

Being involved in school also helped with my self-esteem. I'd read the announcements in the morning with daily quotes. I also loved helping my teachers hand out papers to my peers in class, or with anything in general. This helped me to feel good about myself, because I'd get recognition from the teachers for doing this. It also helped the teachers to believe me when I got bullied and the kids made up things about me, either about what I had said or done, because I was a teacher's pet. "Why would Wynnikka do that? She doesn't act like that? She's respectful," The teachers would say.

Just before high school, I found myself volunteering in the community with many different initiatives, especially when it came to leading youth. Many of my mentors and teachers described me as a positive leader and an advocate for others. I first started by becoming a volunteer youth camp leader in training, with a few other youth in the community. We wouldn't create the schedules and activities for the youth, but we would lead the activities and monitor the youth. This was the same camp where I once attended, which made it easier, because I knew what to expect. I then joined a youth art project initiative, where many local artists came to teach us different visual art forms, such as graffiti, painting, photography, and simple drawings. We used these to create art projects in the community on bridges, murals on the side of the community centre building, and graffiti t-shirts and backpacks for ourselves. Our projects, like face-painting, were photographed and posted in local coffee shops and libraries.

I went on from being a youth in the community programs to

the leader of the programs. We helped to create programming, and implemented them for our young participants. My favourite one of them all was gardening. We were trained in gardening and kitchen safety, then we taught the youth how to plant their own vegetables. Once their vegetables grew, we harvested them and taught them how to cook by showing them how to use the vegetables in their meals. We also put on community movie nights outside once a month, and went on excursions to farms, and went fruit picking. We even took them out for dinner sometimes. Out of all the programs I was a part of, this one was my favourite.

CHAPTER 7

Fresh Start

A fresh start, and on to another level—high school. There were new people everywhere, but I also saw some kids from my old school. They started the rumour that I had kicked two girls' asses in grade eight at our old school, and I definitely confirmed it with pride. I felt pretty nice. I didn't have any bullying issues in high school.

I started off high school great, having my best friend Jae with me in the same school. I convinced her to attend the same high school as me. We met a few other friends throughout our school years, though many of them went their own way after high school. We met our other best friend, Bree, during the second semester of grade ten. I met other friends as well who are now friends for life. Others just became acquaintances.

I was really excited to join the steel pan band in grade nine. Mom told me she used to play, and encouraged me to join regardless of my disability, because there would be a way to adapt and accommodate myself in order to play the instrument. I enjoyed the first week, but I was on the bigger pan drums at the back of the class. I didn't find it fun, because I wanted to play up at the front with the high pitched "ting-ti-ting-ting-ting-di-ni-ni-ni-ning," not the "duh-dum-dum-dim-dum-di-dap-da-dum." Some students had one pan to play and some had two. Our instructor told me I needed to find a way to play both pans, because I had two. I tried holding two sticks between my fingers just in my left hand, but it was hard. I couldn't do it, so I began to give up on the class. I looked around, and everyone was able to play the way the teacher wanted them to. One day, I looked around and stopped trying to play.

The teacher came up to me and said, "Maybe this isn't the class for you, you know?"

I said, "You know what? You're probably right." I walked out of the class without another word, went through the nearest exit of the school, and bawled my eyes out.

Not only did I feel bad that I couldn't play like my mom, but this teacher discouraged me, making me feel as if because I couldn't play like everyone else, I shouldn't keep trying to accommodate myself and stay in the class. I told Mom and Dad that I dropped the class because I didn't really like how the teacher taught us. I just wanted to avoid the confrontation, because I knew exactly how that would have played out. My parents would have gone to the superintendent of the school or the trustee had I told them the exact reason why I dropped the class. I didn't want all of that drama since I was now in high school, so I just joined a drama class instead.

My favourite class was film, because we watched old movies every week and were able to write and act out our own short films. Speaking of acting, drama class was also one of my all-time favourites, and I enjoyed every single assignment we got. There was one kid in my class that I despised. I don't know why we were even friends on Facebook, when in fact we were enemies in real life. We got into little arguments all the time in class, and he started tormenting me on my Facebook page. I usually ignored him, but there was this one night when he crossed me, and I really told him about himself. I went off on him all over Facebook, about everything. The next day, bright and early, I was on time for drama, real drama. As people arrived at class, he was there, and I was laughing with my friends in the class. He walked right up to where I was sitting, and he put his hands around my neck and began choking me. I was in shock. I wasn't even scared really, I just couldn't believe this boy had the actual guts to put his hands around a girl's neck. I squeezed his wrist, and I saw my teacher yelling and sprinting towards us, and she yanked him off of me and pushed him out of the class and called the hall monitor. I showed her what he was doing on Facebook, and what I said. He's the one that ended up getting suspended, of course, and then I deleted him from my Facebook friends list. I shouldn't have even had him on there. It wasn't long before there was a rumour floating around the school, which was so annoying. The following school year we made amends, and I forgave him for what he did. I still see him every now and then, and we greet each other like nothing ever happened years ago. Then again, it was a few years ago, and forgiveness leads to peace of mind.

I remember in grade nine when there were tickets being sold for an upcoming dance, and I guess everyone procrastinated like me and waited until the last day they were being sold to purchase tickets. It was a ridiculous line-up throughout the foyer of the school, and it wasn't even organized, so people kept pushing each other around. I was the fourth person away from the ticket booth, and there was a big guy behind me hovering over me, standing at about 6' 2". He and his friends kept pushing forward hard. I got pissed off and turned around and said, "Stop pushing! You're like the fifth person until the window." He just looked at me, and I turned back around. Two minutes later they started again, and I turned around yelling the same thing. This time he said, "Shut up, bitch, or I'll shank you."

Him threatening to stab me set off every bad nerve in my system, and I was instantly outraged. "Bitch? Are you dumb? Shank who? Me?" It turned into a huge rant about if he ever so much as dared to touch me. Mind you, I was a "niner," not known to many in the school, still quite invisible to the overall student body, and school had only started a month or so before. I got all up in his space, and the hall monitor who knew me came through the crowd and stood in front of me, still allowing me to go off in his face. He resembled a younger version of Shemar Moore and was absolutely gorgeous! The surprising part of it all was that this guy hadn't said one word at all. As I went off in his face, the entire foyer full of over a hundred students was pin-drop silent. I finally stopped, and he just turned around without a word and walked away. All the older students like him came up to me asking if I was good, and telling me how they couldn't believe I had told him off. I didn't get into an altercation with anyone else within the school after that incident. I stood up for myself, and everyone there clearly saw that I, Wynnikka was not playing.

It wasn't long before I had surrounded myself with some more friends, and some were in higher grades than I was. There was a day when we went over to the mall across the street from our high school during lunch hour. I had no idea they were going to steal until we were leaving the store, and I wanted to be cool so I grew brave and stuffed some candy and gum packets up my sleeve and down my track pants like they had done, but I still bought two gum packs and a water bottle. I had never stolen before then, and I felt horrible for doing so, and ended up giving away what I had stolen to some friends. They said if I stole from another store it would prove that I'm not a wuss. At first I refused because I knew better, but they kept calling me out to do it. I didn't want to look like a wuss, so I went into the store, looked right up into the camera like an idiot, and stole perfume right out of the box, then walked out of the store. They were gone! My so-called friends had left me all by myself. I speed-walked towards the exit of the mall, and right before I exited the mall, I felt a tap on my right shoulder. It was a 6' 4" security guard hovering over me, and my first thought was, "Ah damn, just give him back the stolen goods, and he'll let you go." I smiled at him and said, "Yes, sir?" playing like I didn't know why I had gotten stopped by him. He said, "I believe you have something that doesn't belong to you."

I opened my backpack and gave him the perfume and said, "Okay, there you go. Have a great day."

He chuckled. "No, it doesn't work like that. If you don't want to make a huge scene, follow me."

And so I did, fearing for my life.

We walked right back into the store, and he opened a grey metal door that led to a room with a bunch of surveillance TV screens and no windows. He then told me to take a seat. He called for a female employee as a witness and then showed the tape of me stealing the merchandise. I looked so ridiculous. He had her pat me down from head to toe as I stood up, and I was so grateful that she didn't feel the other candy I still had hidden in my pocket. He asked me for a receipt from the dollar store, and I said they didn't give me one. He looked at me in disbelief but proceeded to do paperwork. He called the police and asked me if this was my first offense, and I remember saying, "And last. So, hey, am I getting arrested?"

He said, "If a parent or guardian doesn't come in time for you, I'm afraid so, until they do."

Turns out I had stolen a tester perfume. Not only was it my first offense, but it was also legitimately worthless to have me banned from the mall for an entire year. Mom and Dad had always answered their cell phones or the house phone, but this time I was calling all three, and no one was answering me. I thought I was getting "Punk'd." What if I only got one phone call? They eventually answered, but I had already started with my cow-bawling. Dad came for me, and was way more pissed off than Mom. Mom shrugged it off in my defense, saying it was my first offense, although she was highly disappointed in me. I went into the police station the next day with Dad to do fingerprints and mug shots. I found this so funny and badass, because I was into watching CSI: Crime Scene Investigation and Law & Order at the time, but Dad wasn't having it. I got charged and was ordered to complete fifty hours of community service. I was already heavily involved in community volunteering programs, so I completed those hours very easily. My charges were eventually dropped, and although it was the lightest offense of all, I have never done, and will never do, something like that ever again.

I was a regular teenager who never wanted to do my chores without running to my BlackBerry in the midst of doing my chores, whenever I heard the BBM text tone go off. My parents had to literally take my phone away until my chores were completely done. They still treated me just like any other teenager. They knew I was capable of carefully doing some chores, so whenever I didn't do them when asked, there were strict consequences.

I skipped school a lot in grade nine with friends, to sneak into the same mall I was banned from or the community park nearby, but I was always on top of my work and grades. I was forever handing in assignments late. But when I got to grade ten, regardless of what my friends were doing, I began to buckle down. I skipped class once with my group of girlfriends, to go confront another group of teenage girls from another school, who had called me retarded and made fun of my right arm. No one fought that day; we just stood there arguing, and they continued to make fun of me, and then we just went back to school. I came home that day, and my history teacher had called my mom's cell phone, saying he was worried because I had skipped his class and it was unlike me. I told her why I had almost gotten into a fight, and that I had skipped my afternoon classes to do it. She was proud of me for sticking up for myself, but she didn't like the idea of me skipping class and leaving school property to do it. She told me to stay out of fights all the time, unless someone put their hands on me first. I was grounded for about a week. The next day I got a lecture from my history teacher about it and other lessons in life. He was right, but everything he said was cliché. I just wanted to prove I was tough too, but he said I was a leader and that he had always seen me as such, so he didn't want to hear of me skipping school ever again. I really didn't do anything like that after that day. There was truly no point to prove anything to anyone.

In grade ten, although I was getting an allowance, I wanted to make and spend my own money during school. Mom and Dad always told me to focus on school and not to worry about money until summer. However, some of my friends had already started working and were asking me why I wasn't, so I felt I really needed to. One of my friends told me about this student job opportunity where she would sell chocolates for a company to raise money. It took me a few months to realize that it may have been a scam. They would drive around and place us in front of random franchises and other fancy places downtown, even on beaches, to sell these chocolates without permission from the owners. I didn't know you had to have permission to do so, I was just doing the best job I could. In the middle of winter, we would stand there for eight hours, begging people to buy chocolates, freezing our butts, fingertips, and toes off. We sold these chocolates for $5.00 each, and only made $1.00 off each one, which wasn't fair. We were doing all the dirty work but were getting paid the least. We sometimes received tips, but our driver would manipulate us into handing over half our tips by emptying our clothes. I grew smart and started wearing jeans under my track pants to hide the tips I had received from customers. It wasn't long before my mom found out from other parents what the company was about, and yanked me right out of it. I remember making enough money to buy my own pair of purple and white Nike high-tops, which I took great care of and pride in.

I really didn't think I would have experienced bullying the way I did throughout elementary and middle school, but I did. There was an after-school program for students in the community to attend once a week. There was a small white shuttle bus that picked up participants from our school, then picked up students from two other schools. There was tension between the girls from our school and the girls from the other schools. They were always arguing and insulting each other. This group of girls decided to call out my disability, and was always making fun of me every chance they got. They called me ugly, fat, and retarded, and moved their arms around, being rude and disrespectful. It reminded me of getting bullied in elementary and began to really get to me after a while. I didn't understand why, because I had never bothered anyone, and I minded my own business. I was always nice, so I guess they were just picking on me just to pick on me. There was one day when we were being dropped off after the program, and the group of girls from that one school really went in on my disability, walking up and down the bus calling me names. I remember my phone was dead, but I had these huge earphones and pretended like I wasn't listening to them. They got dropped off first, and as they were coming out, I said something to them, and one girl turned around and said, "Look! At least I can clap with both hands, you retarded bitch." I felt disrespected, and was left there in silence. I got dropped off, and the driver who was a really nice lady didn't open the doors as I walked down the steps of the bus. I looked behind me and shot her a look, but what she said changed my mind-set. She said, "Please don't listen to them. They are a bunch of hooligans, and you are better than them."

I believed her, but those girls clearly weren't done with me yet. During the program, we went on an excursion to a roller skating rink, and everything was cool. I can't really skate, but I was wearing knee and elbow pads, and hadn't fallen. We were getting ready to leave and were taking off our skates. The tables were very easy to wobble, as they were not bolted to the floor. I leaned on one to catch my balance, and with the lightest pressure on it, it tipped over and both my friend and I fell and landed flat on our behinds. Everyone was laughing, but I was trying not to pay attention to them. One of my other friends who was there showed me the next day at school that someone had shared a picture of me after I fell, on Twitter, with the caption, "No one told her fat ass to sit on the table." I wasn't even trying to sit! I was so mad, and I took down her username and told my mom about it. She was furious, so she called my principal. I opened my Twitter and showed it to her. She took a screenshot of the post and sent it to that girl's principal. The girl was suspended and was ordered to complete a few hours of working with special needs children at an elementary school before returning to her school. She kept posting things about me on her Twitter for about a week before she stopped and gave up, because I kept updating my principal, who updated hers, getting her into trouble every time. I didn't care; she and her friends could have called me a snitch all they wanted, but I knew it was the right thing to do until they left me alone.

In grade 11, I wanted to take on a sport, and my pick was rugby. I had a friend at the time who got me into watching football, so it felt really nice to join a similar sport. I was so scared to start playing, because I heard there was at least one serious injury per game, every game, but I wanted to give it a shot. I remember bringing home the form, and I remember the form listing all the possible things that could go wrong that the school wouldn't ever be responsible for, including death. I gave Mom the form to sign, but she refused to sign it, at first. When I asked why, she said, "You know, Nika, rugby is a tough sport. Why don't you play something like badminton? You do have a disability, and of course you should play a sport, but this is putting you at a seriously dangerous risk. What if you get badly hurt? People get concussions, they break limbs, they lose teeth, they get stomped on, they get scratched. What if you get tackled during a very intense game, and someone doesn't realize your arm and hurts it badly, or even breaks it? What if someone steps on your head with their cleats?"

I said, "I know, Mom. I still want to play."

So she warned me, and then proceeded to sign the form. Oh, was I the happiest. I was so excited to get up early in the morning as I needed to be at a 7:00 a.m practice. The first few nights after I started I couldn't sleep. I loved every dreadful, energy-draining practice. We practiced outside in the mud, rain or shine. I loved it. Of course, my coach made some accommodations for me and showed me how to make safe maneuvers when dropping, rolling, going in for a head-on tackle, or taking a hit as a forward. We made it to our first game, an exhibition game at home, and we played to win; and so we did. My favourite part of playing rugby was the huddle or scrum. A couple of practices after that win, we were getting ready for the actual season. During a practice, a teammate tackled me wrong, and all her weight came down on my ankle, and it twisted backwards. It is quite hard to imagine exactly how that went down, but bear with me. I heard and felt it crack. I felt the pain, screamed in agony, and I blacked out for a quick second. When I opened my eyes, I saw my coaches hovering over me. I was still in so much pain, I didn't even want to look at my ankle because I could have sworn it was broken. I was crying, and I started thinking to myself, "Yup, I'm definitely done now. Mom is going to kill me. She knew something like this was going to happen." And to tell you the truth, seventy-five percent of the reason why I kept crying was because I was out for the season, and Mom would never sign a sports form for me ever again. They called Dad to come get me to take me straight to the hospital. They warned me not to take off my cleats until I saw a doctor for an x-ray. Turns out, it was just a sprain that would recover in a matter of weeks. That had me out for the rest of the season, and I was really upset about it. But there was nothing I could've done. It was an accident.

In grade 11 I enjoyed participating in performance shows. I was involved in singing, dancing, and other random performances like youth art initiatives and the multicultural shows. These are the moments I cherished about high school. I truly don't remember anything in terms of workload, but I remember all my fun and memorable experiences along with the bad ones that taught me valuable life lessons.

Remember one of my best friends I told you about earlier who moved away in grade two? He ended up coming to my grade eleven fitness class, and I didn't recognize him at first. He was hovering over me this time, instead of being shorter than me, and he was all bearded up, covering his baby face. He eventually shaved it off, and I was like "Yup. Nothing changed but the facial hair growth." I thought he was so cute, along with some of the other girls in the class who got all googly-eyed when he spoke to them. One day, we were working on machines right beside each other, and I knew he was working out beside me, but I kept coaching myself to keep my eyes forward and not to make awkward eye contact with him. He randomly asked me something, and I looked to see if he was actually talking to me, because I don't think we had exchanged words before then. I said to myself, "Is this fine guy for real talking to me right now?" Then I replied to him, "Me?" And he said, "Yeah," then asked if I knew who he was because he remembers me very well. I just looked at him like he was nuts. He tried to get me to remember him by saying his name and the school we went to when we were younger, and it took me a few seconds to process that who was sitting beside me was my "brother from another mother." My best friend from grade two. I jumped up so fast off the machine and screamed his full name. What a moment, man, nine years overdue. We smiled and gave each other a big hug. We caused a scene in the class, causing everyone to stare at us for a brief moment, puzzled, until we explained what all that was for. I felt gross afterwards for having a crush on my brother for two weeks, which disappeared in an instant once I knew who he really was. He was my "batty (bottom) and bench," "two peas in a pod," until he changed schools a few months later, disappearing again, but we connected on Facebook and exchanged numbers, so he wasn't lost from me this time. I still see him from time to time.

When I graduated from high school, I received a scholarship, many leadership awards, and graduated with honours—I received an eighty-six percent GPA. It was a wonderful feeling. I also completed 120 hours of community volunteer hours, when the required amount was just forty. I realized once I got to college that forty was nothing compared to 700 plus hours of co-op. Before I graduated, the college I was going to was down the street from my school, so during my spare periods in the afternoon I'd leave to go get lost in the college and find out where everything was, so I was ahead and prepared by the time I became a student there.

I was actually upset with our high school because, for our grade twelve commencement night, we didn't wear caps and gowns, though the teachers and the principals were all sitting and wearing blue and yellow caps and gowns. I just found it extremely odd. I was looking forward to tossing my cap in the air and prancing around the auditorium like a *High School Musical* remake, but no. I did, however, wear a set for my college graduation, but there was no throwing of the caps or flinging of the gowns.

CHAPTER 8

Transitioning Into College

When I finally started college in September 2013, I was eager to begin the new endeavour. I had already figured out the ins and outs of the school throughout the previous year and over the summer. I also found out that there was a centre specifically for students with disabilities on campus, and they really helped me to ease into my first college school year. I utilized their space to complete work in their computer lab, and I didn't have to wait on anyone to get off before I could use a computer. Instead of sitting up at a computer on a hard chair I could find a comfy place somewhere around the school with my laptop or loaner laptop from the library and finish my assignments. I also had notetakers to assist me when taking notes was too much for me. In school, I found it better to type out my notes rather than writing them out. I ended up going through a lot in college; especially the fall semester after my mother's passing earlier on in the year. I couldn't focus as much as I used to, and I wasn't completing my assignments on time. I was in co-op placement in the fall, just after school had started, and I remember sitting in the intake room, in dim lighting, about four hours after my shift had ended, contemplating suicide. I was thinking about killing myself by jumping in front of a train instead of going home. I felt I had had enough. In that same moment, my brother called me crying, saying that he missed Mom and he didn't know what to do anymore. And it hit me hard. I realized then that if I were to commit suicide, I wouldn't just be affecting my life, I would be affecting my entire family's life. It would be selfish to them. What would happen to my brother and my sister who loved and cared about me? They didn't have a mother figure, and, sure, I was only nineteen, but it was I who fell next in line. Yes, our father was the head of the household, but he needed me too. He needed my support with them as well. So I took the subway home and gave everyone a big hug, a big group hug. My family and I, we are a unit, and we each play an important role in holding this family together. Every day we hug each other and say, "I love you."

I always knew the importance of applying for grants and bursaries, as well as searching around for them, because many were available but were not well advertised to students. I made sure to continue to search for more and apply way before their due dates. In 2011, when I was in grade eleven, I received a bursary award for college and at the award ceremony there was a guest speaker by the name of Tamara Gordon. She spoke of her life story, which truly inspired me. She had a deep passion for playing many sports, especially basketball, winning many medallions and awards. In 2002, she was severely injured during a school skiing trip, which left her paralyzed from the waist down. She did not allow her disability to stop her, and I remember her saying "I am confined to my wheelchair but thank God! My mind is free! My mind is not restricted because of my body!" Hearing this really touched me, and inspired me to be great regardless of the fact I had a physical limitation. I really wanted to speak to her before the ceremony was over. After they had served our meals, I looked around for her and went up to her to give her a big hug. I told her how much her story meant to me, and as we conversed, she mentioned that she also suffered from Brachial Plexus Injury, and I couldn't believe my ears. She was the first person I had ever met with a Brachial Plexus Injury, except she sustained it during an accident that hadn't occurred at birth. I went into sharing my disability and my story, which inspired her as well. She also mentioned at the time that she was working on creating a scholarship that would help students with physical disabilities across Ontario with their post-secondary education. She urged me to keep in touch to get updates on when to apply. Fast-forward to mid-2014, when I applied for the scholarship and received it. I was extremely grateful for it, because it helped to take care of some school expenses, aside from tuition, while what I had received from student loans helped with other living expenses. This was crucial, because after losing my mother that year, there was a lot of financial responsibility placed on me. It was no longer just "I'm taking care of myself alone and my own bills." I now had to consider my home, contribute a lot more, and learn self-discipline with budgeting. I reapplied for the scholarship the following school year of 2015, which was my third year of college, and I received it once again.

After my mother passed away, Tammy reached out to support my family and I. She also attended my mother's funeral and I appreciated Tammy even more than I had before. She has become such a great friend of mine over the years and she continues to inspire me. I became an ambassador of her scholarship foundation. I recently spoke at her first ever fundraising Gala to let others know how much the foundation means to me and how much the scholarships have helped me with my studies.

Late in 2014, I was going through a lot, because my boyfriend of almost a year, whom I was actually in love with, had broken up with me a month before our one-year anniversary. He felt that he needed to focus more on himself. He said I hadn't done anything wrong at all and that I was really good to him. I couldn't

Tammy & I Sharing a moment after the first fundraising Gala for the Tamara Gordon Scholarship Foundation

Photo credit: Owen Bucknor

Me speaking at the Fundraising Gala

Photo credit: Owen Bucknor

understand, but I had had enough of that year. It was just taking so much out of me. He was very supportive, loving, and caring. It took me a few months to get over it, but it still hurt, because I never understood why we had to go out like that. I wasn't a distraction. If he needed his space, I would have given it to him. I wasn't clingy, and I never bombarded him with my issues, so I wasn't sure why we had to let go. I just let him go and said "Whatever" to the whole situation, and gave myself some time before I began dating again.

It wasn't until one of my professors approached me after noticing the decline in my grades that I actually let him in on what was happening with me. I remember him telling me the importance of coming forward earlier with things like that, because it wasn't as if he didn't understand that life happens. Coming forward allowed me to be supported more by faculty and to have extra time to get my work done. I started turning to a counsellor at the Centre for Students with Disabilities on a weekly basis, and spoke to him about what I was going through. It really helped to ease my mind most of the time knowing his support was there. He did everything he could to ensure that I was on the right path academically and that I would be successful in graduating on time. I talked out some other things I was going through at the same time as well, which also helped me a lot.

In college, I met a lot of great people and made some great

friends. To be honest, I don't really talk to as many people as I did before I graduated college, but I did meet one of my best friends there and we graduated from the same program together. We used to hit the gym during school time, and it was really fun. College was an amazing experience, and when there were things going on around the campus, I'd try my best to get involved to make the most out of my college experience—spirit days, contests, celebrity events, talent shows, dances, and much more. I don't miss the workload and textbook costs, but I really miss the supportive professors, the friends I made, and the goofy stuff. I even miss going for a Timmy's coffee with classmates during breaks and running back to class.

I really enjoyed my program. There was a lot of networking within the program, which taught me the importance of liaising with many other people and organizations. I appreciate everything about what the program had to offer. I learned a lot and obtained certifications for things such as CPR and First Aid, High FIVE and High FIVE QUEST for Children, Snoezelen training, food handler's training, and "Introduction to Autism training". These I have for life, and nothing but the First Aid CPRC expires every few years.

After graduating from Recreation and Leisure Services, I jumped into Child and Youth Care Services (CYC) the following September. The main reason why I did this was that while at my co-op placement at a shelter as a Recreationist, I developed the ability to connect with the youth and help them on a CYC level. When I asked one of my supervisors about the possibility for employment after the placement, he told me that they loved having me there but unfortunately my Rec and Leisure diploma won't get me the position, since any staff in the shelter could've come up with Rec and Leisure activities. At first, I was beyond offended, but then he suggested going into CYC, because I did have a passion for working with children and youth. Therefore, I took on the program. Three months into my second semester, I dropped out of the CYC program because I was under too much pressure being in school, having co-op placement at an elementary school, and having to travel far back and forth to work at a movie theatre, which was another stressful situation all by itself.

There were times when I wanted to just quit my theatre job, but it would have killed me on the inside. How would I have supported myself for school? I knew I would have had an overload trying to balance school, work, and co-op, plus trying to take care of myself and my family. The schedules collided when I tried to do it all at once, and I began to have anxiety at times. I called 9-1-1 for myself after work one night at 2:00 a.m., because I had an anxiety attack for the first time after feeling chest pains as a result of stress. When the paramedics came and told me what it was and said that my blood pressure was "in better shape than theirs," I just stayed home and took it easy then went to bed.

I was also interested in cosmetology—hair, nails, and make-up—something fun, artistic, and beautiful. The reality for me was that I thought I couldn't do it. I usually got frustrated from not being able to do certain things within the field independently even trying on myself or family members. I've had to change which career path I really wanted to travel on after weighing out the pros and cons of many I was interested in. I've recently found my passion for advocating on behalf of others like myself. I've made it a priority to get involved in initiatives and work that allow me to do so. Just because I have a physical disability, it does not mean that I won't try to live life to the best of my ability.

CHAPTER 9

Coping with a Major Loss

I forgot to say, "I Love You..."

One very important lesson I learned growing up was to say "I love you" to family members and give them a big hug when leaving the house, going to bed, and say it when hanging up the phone, because you don't know if that'll be the last chance you get to do so. My mother began to get sick and show symptoms on the Wednesday before she passed, but to everyone's understanding, she was just coming down with a cold, at least that's what it looked like, so we treated her as such and took care of her. By the following Friday she was just in her bed, wasn't eating, and refused to go see a doctor. I was helping my boyfriend at the time all day that Friday with some work, and was going to go see my goddaughter in the hospital right after, who had been born that morning. Mommy called me to ask me to come home, and I asked her how she was feeling, if everything was okay, and what was the urgency. She didn't give me much of a reason, and when I said, "You know, Mom, everyone's home with you. I still have things to do. I'll be another few hours, but I'll —" she cut me off and said, "You know what, Nika, I'll let you choose, okay? You know where your priorities are."

I couldn't understand what in the world was going on. I was oblivious to the fact that everyone else was home helping to look after her, but she just wanted me there. I didn't know I was going to lose my mother soon. I was kind of bummed that I couldn't finish helping my boyfriend with his work nor see my newborn goddaughter, but I knew I had to go home to be with my mom. I went home and laid beside her, talking to her for a while until she fell asleep, kissed her on her forehead, then got up to get prepared to facilitate a youth volleyball event at the community centre down the street the following day.

Saturday morning, I had a doctor's appointment to wear a heart rate monitor for the rest of the weekend, because I kept having frequent heart palpitations (fluttering), and it began to worry me. The whole weekend I was just supposed to rest and let the monitor get an accurate reading of my heart rate. I went back home, and it was about 1:00 p.m. I went to show mommy the monitor on my chest, and she didn't even turn over to look at me, she just nodded. Dad then told me that Mom didn't look good at all. I just hugged and kissed her. An hour went by, mind you, the tournament was starting in two hours, and I was doing everything I could to ensure that she was doing okay before I left. Dad stopped me as I was putting my shoes on and insisted that I stay home, so I did, and called my co-worker to tell her what was happening and that I couldn't come to the tournament. I felt bad because I'm the type of person who hates to let down people who were depending on me, but everyone knew where I needed to be. In that same moment, Dad was trying to ask Mom questions. She was taking a long time to respond and kept mumbling something. She hadn't eaten anything all day, and kept refusing anything but water. My brother was out with his friend at the time and I called him to come home immediately. Dad then told me something went wrong, and I turned on the light. I looked her in her eyes and said, "Mommy...Mom...what's your name? Mom...what's going on? Mom..."

I helped to get her to sit up, then I let her go. Her eyes began rolling back. That was the scariest thing I had ever seen. She started tilting, unable to hold herself up, and I nearly lost it. Instead of losing it, I knew I had to stay calm. I held her up and I kept talking to her. Then she said her name, answering the question I had asked her a few minutes prior. I yelled out to my dad to hold her up while I found her purse and clothes to go to the hospital. She focused her eyes back on me, and I kept talking to her until Dad came back over to us to help. We were going to bring her to the hospital ourselves, and she had the strength to sit there and tell us not to bring her, pushing us away and trying to fight us not to bring her to the hospital.

I said, "Mom, it's either this or we are calling 9-1-1. You aren't well; let's go."

She still refused, so I reached for my phone while my father helped her to get dressed. I ruffled through her purse for her health card while calling 9-1-1, and made my sister go into her room. My heart was racing fast, my hands started shaking, and I stopped feeling my feet under me.

On the inside, I was already screaming and crying in fear like a child, but I felt I had to be very mature and calm for everyone else. The paramedics took forever to arrive, and I was upset. They kicked us all out of the room and did whatever they were supposed to do. I told her she'd be fine and not to worry, we were right there. I was so concentrated on helping her to gather her things and keeping her up by talking to her that I forgot to say "I love you." After they took her away, I knew she was going to come home. She left in the ambulance around 5:30 p.m., and Dad went with her. The chief paramedic came back for his ambulance, and I ran to ask him before he drove off, "Hey! How's my mom doing?"

"Well, we don't know. We brought her in, but she doesn't look good. Hopefully, it isn't too late."

"Too late?" I snapped.

He said, "Yes, I am sorry."

I just started crying, and ran back home to my brother and sister. I couldn't believe my ears. I just thought he was talking pure bullshit. I sat on the couch, knowing my mom was coming home the same night or the next morning, but at the back of my mind I had a bit of doubt. Maybe she would have to stay there a bit longer, because she was very sick, but she was coming home. My sister was oblivious, still playing with her toys in her room, and she came and asked me what happened to Mom. I told her, "Mommy isn't feeling well. She will be okay; she'll be home soon." I called my father's phone about an hour later, and he wouldn't answer. He called me back a few moments later, and I didn't even say hello, I just yelled, "How's Mom?" What I heard next had me on my knees bawling instantly, feeling as if someone had punched me hard in my stomach and began choking me. I couldn't breathe...I kept gasping for air.

"Mom...Mom is on life support, Nika."

"WHAT?"

"Tell your brother now. Bye, I have to go now. I love you guys. Hug them for me." Click.

I had never heard anything so devastating in my life. I called one of my friends to come over, because I was in panic mode and so was my brother. She came over and played games with our sister and helped to keep my brother calm. I called my boyfriend's mother, crying, barely able to catch my breath, and she said a prayer with me over the phone while trying to calm me down. The rest of the night, I just sat there in shock. It was about 2:00 a.m., and my eyes were red and sore. I was feeling tired, but I couldn't sleep. My friend, brother, and sister had already fallen asleep, and then I finally fell asleep around 3:00 a.m.

It wasn't very long before I woke up again around 6:30 a.m. I called Dad's phone, and he answered. "Nika? You there?"

"Yes, Dad, what's up with Mom? What happened to her?"

"I don't know. She doesn't look good at all."

"I know! But what happened to her?"

“I don’t even know. They keep calling these codes.”

“Dad, what codes?” I was thinking numbers, not colours. All I knew was that “Code Blue” was a heart attack, and he wasn’t being specific enough with me or giving me enough details, so I started getting really upset.

“Nika, I have to call you later. They just called me to look at something. I will call you back. Bye, I love you guys.”

I couldn’t help at that point thinking what life would be like without my mother, and I tried kicking the thought out of my head. I couldn’t go back to sleep at that point. I just stayed up thinking, panicking, worrying, you name it. I just knew my mother was in a really bad state on life support in the hospital. The suspense of her state was killing me on the inside. Almost one hour later, the house phone in the living room rang, and my brother got to it first. He picked up the phone, and I was walking towards him when I saw his jaw drop. He collapsed forward onto the kitchen floor, not saying a word. I picked up the phone, and my friend was now woken up and standing behind me. “Dad, what did you just say to him? DAD!”

“Nika, Mom passed away at 7:05 a.m. It’s 7:25 a.m. now.”

The codes were in fact code blues in the ICU, and they kept reviving her throughout the night, until there was no bringing her back. It just kept going downhill every time. The scream that came from my body took all the power I had away from me. I don’t remember feeling my body when I screamed a long “No.” I was numb, and I dropped onto the floor. For a quick moment, I forgot where I was, who I was, what I was doing. I felt as if something had been ripped right out of my chest, and I threw a full-on toddler tantrum. If I think about it, I can still hear that scream play over again in my mind. Same for our brother; he says he can still hear me, because it was so loud right beside him, screeching almost. My heart was pounding. I felt as if I had been stabbed in my chest a million times, an excruciating pain that would never go away. I was in disbelief. My friend helped me up, and I remember my sister coming out of her room half asleep with her hands over her ears. I just grabbed her and my brother and stood there crying. My brother ran upstairs to our family friend to get her, and she was crying, but waited with us. My godmother came to drive us to the hospital. When we got there, we speed-walked through the ICU. The curtains got drawn back, and we saw her there with tubes and tanks hooked up to her, but she was already gone. I felt as if I was in a really bad nightmare, and I just wanted someone to wake me up. It was so unreal. We started screaming and crying. I was hovering over her, hugging and kissing her cold face. "Mommy! I'm sorry. I love you! I'm so sorry! No! I'm sorry! Why? Mommy, I'm sorry." I was just sorry.

I held my sister and brother and kept crying. We saw our father sitting and crying in the chair in the farthest corner of the room, and he stood up to hug us. I looked back at the monitor, and saw a huge white "0" with a green flat line. She was gone for real and forever. She was sleeping and wasn't going to wake up ever again. Our father just held us there. Everyone started arriving, and a few of us left to go speak to the doctor who was dealing with her so he could explain everything. He told us what had happened. He also said that we shouldn't focus on "what ifs" and "what could have been," it wouldn't do anything for us but make us more upset and lengthen the healing process. I hated hearing that, but he was right. We had to move forward and figure out what to do next now that she was gone. We had to figure out how we were going to live without Mom. It was sudden, she had always been there, and in an instant she was gone without notice or preparation. We will never hear her voice again, see her smile, hear her laugh. At that point, I would've given anything to see her smile again or hear her scold me for not washing the dirty dishes when she asked me to, right then and there. I felt like a huge baby. I just wanted to cry and cry and keep crying. When we got home, my eyes were red and itchy. She died on a very sunny, clear-skied Sunday morning. She was happy and at peace, smiling. She is our guardian angel now. Some family and friends and my boyfriend at the time came over to visit and help comfort us. I went into her room and saw her red robe and the hat she wore to the hospital folded on her bed, and I began crying all over again. It was over, and she was gone for good, but I hadn't accepted it nor did it hit me, even after seeing her being taken away at the hospital. Even after being there to make funeral arrangements, even after her funeral, it was just so unreal to me. Of course, it was real, but in my heart it didn't become a reality for me for months. We had a lot of support from family and friends. Some of our community leaders, teachers, professors, and even principals came around to morally support us.

A few weeks before she passed away she had said, "Nika, I want to live to see my grandchildren."

I looked at her like she was crazy before responding to her statement. I said, "Mom, you will! What kind of mad talk is that? You're young, and you will be the best grandmother ever. I know you'll spoil them so much that I'll get super-jealous and wish you were my grandmother. Ha-ha. Nothing is baking in this oven for the next few years well. Not to worry, you will. What exactly makes you think you won't live to see them, Mom?"

"I don't know, Nika."

I didn't understand. I just smiled, then gave her a big hug and told her I loved her. I just thought she needed some sort of validation. Mothers, you are doing a wonderful job. You are amazing, you are strong. Don't doubt yourself, you are doing your best.

She always asked us if we loved her. Again, I'd look at her like she lost her mind somewhere outside on her way home from work. I'd just hug and kiss her and say, "Obviously, I do!"

"But why do you love me, Nika?"

"Are you serious, Mom? I just do. We all do. You're the best mom ever. You love us, you nurture us, you and Dad have raised us well, and you care for us so much. And you're funny. You're the coolest mom. Everyone says that!"

She'd just smile back at me. She always had these "If I were to die tomorrow" lines that were excellent to know but worried me. For example, "If were to die tomorrow, life goes on, dear John, keep continuing to live your life. I'm already gone, and you must live." She also turned to Dad one day and said, "If I were to die tomorrow, don't worry, Nika will take care of everything and make sure you guys' heads are on straight, and keep you guys in check. Ha-ha." She made a joke out of it, but he took it very hard. I remember him getting mad at her, because he couldn't believe she was talking like that, as if she knew something was bound to happen to her soon. Sometimes I wonder if she knew she was going to pass away and just didn't want to tell us to scare us. I wish she had told us about the pain she was in so we could do something to help. But what if there was nothing we could've done? At this point, I believe there was nothing we could've done, and she wanted us to live without worrying. I used to wonder if it was our fault for not seeing her more. Did we take her presence for granted? I don't think so. We miss her so much now, and not a day goes by that we don't think about her.

The following week Monday, I jumped right into my very first summer job as a field worker, doing community clean-ups, gardening, cleaning underground garages, window washing, wall washing, cleaning buildings while wearing bed bug suits, organizing storage closets, cleaning out housing apartments, and more. On my first day, I remember telling people why I started a week late in the youth summer job program, and they thought I was crazy to be there with them working just one week after losing my mother, and not taking time to grieve. I just shrugged and said, "I know what I have to do. It's mandatory that I start working right away to help support my family. Unfortunately, I have no other choice right now." Aside from the gardening, it was definitely a gross job, and I was putting myself at risk in major ways, but I never made excuses, because I knew what I had to do. It was a lot on my disability, completing repetitive tasks, especially with my left hand, for six to eight hours. My left arm would be sore and in pain, as well as my neck and shoulders. Not to mention my back. I have scoliosis as well, so the standing all day and bending to sweep and mop were hard on my body, but then again, I never complained because I felt as if I had no other choice. The greatest thing about the job was that not only was it family oriented, but also on Wednesdays all groups, from East to West, got together for workshops, led by staff and guest speakers, that taught us about work etiquette, professionalism, and budgeting, amongst other things.

My previous supervisor is now one of my mentors and like a second mother to me. She is such an amazing woman. She and one of my other supervisors, continue to reach out to my family sharing wonderful opportunities with us, and are always asking us to participate. I'm always eager to do so, especially because I know and understand the importance of taking on new opportunities and networking with many different people to enhance my future.

I'm an overprotective big sister to my siblings. My siblings and our father are my heart. Before my mother passed away, she would give me certain responsibilities so I would be able to take care of them, and then when I did something for them without her asking, she used to say, "Nika, you are such a mother hen." Then she would laugh. After losing Mommy, it was a bit easier for me to jump into the role of being an authoritative, motherly figure to them, while remaining in the role of their sister. Dad was doing his part and extra, but I really felt I needed to step up, because they no longer had a mother.

I ensure they are on top of their school work, check in on their day, and attend school meetings with Dad. It's hard, yes, but I'm getting through it. There are times when they get into an argument over something small, and I have to be a mini-mediator between them, and have them understand each other, apologize, and forgive each other. There are other times when I literally have to get them where it hurts for not listening or for not doing their chores—shutting down the Wi-Fi. Yes, I would change the Wi-Fi password as often and as long as was needed in order to get them to do what they were supposed to do. And you can bet when they couldn't log on to the Wi-Fi that they would get on top of whatever needed to be done.

There were many times while working that my mother's passing came across my mind, and I had the urge to cry. I suppressed the emotion every time and continued to work. There was one time when I couldn't, and I just asked my supervisor for permission to go home that day, and she let me go, no questions asked. Everyone there was supportive. I really enjoyed the program, but I had just lost my mom, and had to act as if nothing had happened most of the time to keep pushing and get my work done. I didn't have enough time to properly grieve her passing. Some family and friends helped at first, but I just had to keep working.

After my mother's passing, I experienced more stress and anxiety than I'd ever experienced in my entire life. I was always thinking and overthinking about what needed to be done right and what didn't go right. I had more responsibilities at home—worrying about bills, groceries, emergencies, on top of taking care of my own health. I was under a lot of pressure that year, from losing my mother and being in my last year of college, to my boyfriend breaking up with me because he felt he needed to focus on himself. Also, I've noticed that I've become anxious about my health since my mother passed away. If something is wrong with me, I quickly run to a doctor to be checked out. Sometimes my friends feel as if I'm just worrying too much and even went as far as to comparing me to the giraffe in the movie Madagascar, but I am terrified of neglecting my health and having something bad happen to me. I'd rather be safe than sorry.

There are major challenges to adjust to our new way of living without our mom being here. I remember receiving Facebook messages almost every night from my mom while she was at work. She would send affirmations reminding us about how special we were to her and our father, and how loved we were. I appreciated those messages, and even more now, because now I just scroll up through our old conversations whenever I feel confused, upset, happy, sad, depressed, or lonely. Whenever I read them, it's almost as if I can still hear her talking to me.

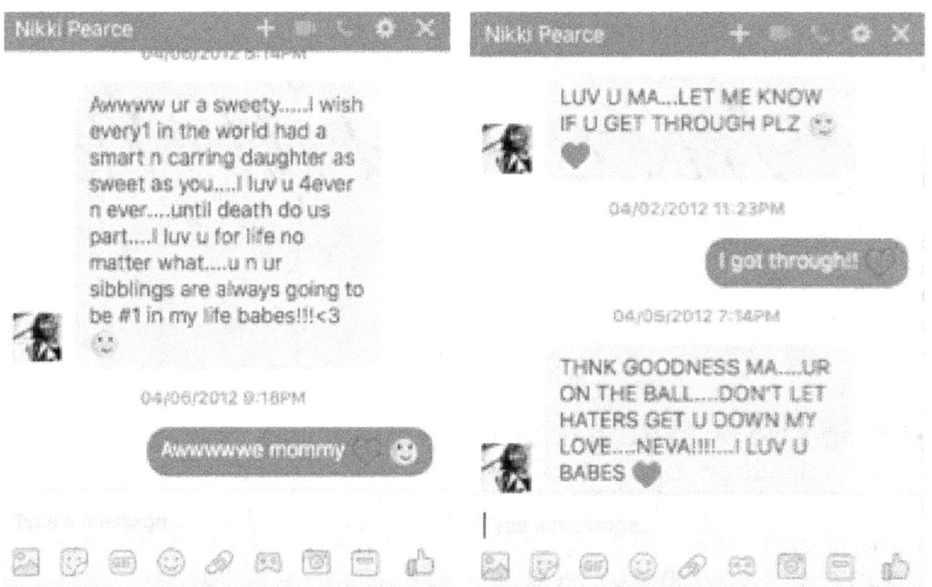

I have learned so much from having to go through this experience, and I'm still learning. It is so important to say what you have to say and do what you're supposed to do in life. Lead by example, and love and appreciate those you have around you: family, friends, mentors, elders, coworkers, neighbours, and acquaintances. You never know what tomorrow holds. At some point, you'll experience a loss if you haven't already, but you can make sure you are semi-prepared by doing the above. Make sure that before you leave this earth and return to your Creator you do your best to live your life the best way you can. Show gratitude towards others who help and support you. Hold no grudges and keep no enemies; nothing is an enemy unless you allow it to be. Don't internalize everything you hear or see about yourself. A wise person once said that a ship only sinks because of the amount of water that gets in. Take care of yourself first, physically, mentally, emotionally, and spiritually. If you don't, and something happens to you, how will you then be able to take care of everything else that requires your attention? Do the things you love and enjoy every moment. Don't just be alive and breathing, live your life to the fullest.

CHAPTER 10

I'm Ashamed of Me

Because of how the kids my age made me feel about myself all the time, almost every day, for years, I still carry that way of thinking sometimes, especially when I go out with my friends to a party where we have to mix and mingle with random people. I always try to wear something that hides my arm like an oversized scarf or shawl. Something that has pockets, like a light jacket or jumpsuit works too so that I can hide my arm and not have to worry about someone laughing at me or posting my disability on their social media. It's one thing to feel insecure about being the biggest one of your friends, but to have a disability too is a double whammy, and sometimes I don't feel like going out. Of course, they'd convince me to go out eventually, and they'd encourage me to have more confidence in myself, and not let others' ignorance and disrespect discourage me from going out and having a great time with them. They hated when I felt this way, because they didn't see a problem with me. But it's when we go out and they get approached sometimes and I don't that I start to wonder why.

I also noticed that whenever we went out and I hid my arm, I got approached more. It's sad, but then again, why would I want an asshole who can't fully accept me for who I am, or is "embarrassed" of me anyways? My mother was a fashion police, so I've always known how to put myself together quite nicely. I'd look in the mirror and think to myself "Okay, Nika, so you're a big girl? No problem. Get dolled up and slay, honey." My mom forever slayed when she got ready, no matter what it was, and she was full-figured, so she showed me the ropes. "Do colour coordinate; do not mix two different patterns; do not wear tight fitting clothes; do wear earrings always; do not wear anything "short up" on you and do accessorize."

Dating is supposed to be fun, of course, but it can also be nerve-wracking, especially during the first encounter after meeting someone online. Meeting partners online is the norm in today's society, whether it is through social media, such as Facebook, Twitter, Instagram, or an online dating site. I do not like going out on first dates sometimes, because I have a bit of anxiety over how they'll react to my physical disability, even if I have already explained it to them before the first date. I usually hide my disability at first, and I always have to think of the best time to reveal it to them, like it's a huge problem when it really isn't. The earlier the better. I've always wondered, but have never asked, if when I explained my disability to them over the phone before we met for the first time, and they thought they had a clear understanding or an idea of what it looked like, if when they saw it in person they thought it was worse than what they initially anticipated. Some would stop talking to me. If they were truly interested in me, they'd have to accept me, all of me. I know you're probably wondering if I even had a picture on my profile of myself, exposing my physical disability. Absolutely not. My reasoning? I was being cautious. Sure, I have full-body photos online, but the internet is such a cruel place, and people do mean things like screenshot and share within seconds, or create memes. I felt it would be embarrassing for me and that no one would bother talking to me if they saw it. Due to my experience with bullying, I hide my arm in photos from the fear of being judged or mocked. I'm constantly fighting myself with this. It's personal, and causes anxiety sometimes, so I'd rather not show it and just explain what had happened in person.

Now, would that count as catfishing? No. I'm still the same person they saw in the picture, there's just something about me that I haven't revealed to them as yet. No guy has ever seen me in person, on a date, and had the audacity to disrespect me for having a noticeable disability. They've all seemed okay with it, but I guess I've always had a preconceived notion of them being embarrassed, so I'd hide it. But why should I continue to put myself through such worries? I want to eventually meet someone who sees me for me, all of me. Someone who sees beyond my limitations and wants to know more about me; not that they don't care about it, but it isn't all they see in me, because I am more than just my physical disability.

Everyone who sees me and knows me says that I give off a vibe that I have confidence in myself, but I am a work in progress. When I go out on a date for dinner, I avoid ordering anything that requires cutting food with a knife and fork, such as chicken breast or steak. Sometimes I'd forget and order something that requires cutting, and when it comes I'd have to take the knife by itself and start cutting it without any support from a fork to hold it in place. If the food was a bit chewy or tougher to cut, I'd show obvious signs of struggle, but I'd keep at it until it worked. Sometimes I'd just give up and I wouldn't finish; I'd just sit there eating what was cut and leave the rest of the food. I don't ever ask for help, and if they'd offer their help I'd say I'm okay, but if they insisted, I'd let them. My ex-boyfriend and I went out for dinner downtown in the late winter season once, and I remember the restaurant had some sort of retro feel to it. We were seated and began ordering our food. There was a steak dish that sounded very appealing, and I ordered it, forgetting that I may have a problem cutting it. We conversed, laughing and talking until our food came. When our waitress placed my plate down in front of me, that's when it hit me, and hit me really hard. "Shit! Can I even cut this? He's never seen me cut anything with one hand. Will he be embarrassed of me? Breathe and just start cutting." I began cutting, and just my luck, the steak was a bit hard to cut through. He looked up at me and said, "Hey, you want me to cut it? Why didn't you just ask for help?" I told him I was fine, still struggling to move the knife through the steak, and he replied "Here, it's okay, let me do it." This seemed like something small and nothing I should feel ashamed about, but after I pushed my plate towards him and he looked down, I started to silently cry while watching him cut it. I was just very embarrassed and felt that he probably felt sorry for me. I went back to hating the fact that I had a disability and hating the doctor that did this to me, for a brief moment. He shouldn't have had to do that, but he still did, and I accepted that. It didn't seem as if he was embarrassed by it, so what was my deal? I just felt horrible. I wiped my tears before he looked up and he pushed my plate back in my direction. I was at the brink of losing my appetite, but I still ate my dinner, and it was really good. He never knew I cried, and I never told him.

The same thing happens to me when I go out for dinner with friends, but I never tell them no, I always allow them to do it for me if they insist after I say I am fine and it looks like I'm not. I just don't want them feeling sorry for me. I know they just want to help, but I feel babied sometimes, and it isn't their fault nor mine.

Warning folks, it's about to get very personal, possibly "TMI" for you. But I like to keep it real, so brace yourselves.

I always feel ashamed of my body, especially naked when I see my arm. Not only am I a "big girl", but I also have a noticeable physical disability. I had to put embarrassment behind me and swallow my pride before becoming intimate with my boyfriend at the time. It was hard, because I still felt embarrassed. I'm sure all women and men have some sort of insecurity about themselves before they get intimate with their partner, and have to put it behind them. My disability was major for me, because I was already a bit embarrassed by my size. Flab and rolls here and there. I thought to myself, "Ugh, what is he going to think? I feel so FAT. OMG look at my arm! Well, this is embarrassing; maybe I can just say I'm sick. Maybe I should keep my dang shirt on. Better yet, keep the lights off and not tell him the real reason why I'd rather have them off. Yeah, we'll turn them off." Did he care? No. Was it in the way? No. So why did I care so much? I was just insecure about having to reveal myself. I wanted to not feel ashamed of myself, but figuring out how to get to that state of mind was the hardest part. Eventually, I felt that the best thing to do was to talk to him about it. I did. I mentioned how I felt about my body, and that I was embarrassed about my arm, and how I felt he thought about me. Not just at that time, but in general. Was he embarrassed of my arm when we walked together on the street and my arm wasn't tucked away in my sleeve or in a pocket somewhere? His response was laughter. I have a bit of anxiety, so I started playing mind-reader and became embarrassed while panicking on the inside in fear of what he'd say next. "Stupid arm...I'm so fat...I knew it." I was already presuming what he thought, but what came out of his mouth next interrupted my thoughts.

"Nika, I can't believe you actually think I'd care." At first I was a bit offended. Not sure if it was because he cared enough not to care about my disability, or because he didn't care at all about my disability. "I do, but I don't. That doesn't matter to me, and you shouldn't have to feel as though it does." Even though hearing that from him was comforting, I was still cautious when going out with him, thinking that others would be staring at my arm and wondering why he was with me. This feeling came from deep within when that boy told me when I was younger that no one would ever like me because of my disability and my weight. Social norms also affect my thinking, so overcoming that mentality with self-love, positive self-talk, and self-acceptance is still a work in progress.

Mom would always make me wear sleeveless dresses to outings and all my graduations. Although I pleaded with her in grade six to let me wear sleeves, she told me that neither she nor Dad would allow me to remain embarrassed of myself and that I must show others that I love myself by not hiding a very special part of me. As much as I disagreed, I still wore the sleeveless dress. At my grade eight graduation, I put up no fight and wore a sleeveless red blouse and black fancy skirt with little red heels. I had a red and cream corsage that I wore on my right wrist especially, because I wanted to draw attention to my right arm on purpose. In grade twelve, I did the same thing again, wearing a sleeveless peplum dress, and I felt most confident in accepting my seven awards, my college scholarship for that year, and most importantly my grade twelve diploma. I wore a nice long blue dress for my grade twelve prom that was sleeveless as well. Unfortunately, I did not go with a date, and neither did my friends, so we went as a clique. I didn't slow dance with any guy to an old school *Love & Basketball* movie track, and I've still yet to do so.

A woman I recently liaised with has a physical disability similar to mine, and she added me to her Facebook page. She's from an organization in Grenada that advocates for those with diverse types of disabilities similar to what I do. I saw that she had gone through some of my pictures and liked a few. A couple of hours later, she messaged me and asked me how come I didn't have any pictures of my arm up on Facebook. This hit me hard: very hard. It brought me back to when my mother lectured me about not hiding my arm and disability. It brought me back to my grade six, eight and twelve graduations, when she made me wear sleeveless dresses to embrace my disability, regardless of how embarrassed I felt. I took heed on my own when I graduated from college and wore a sleeveless dress. Because wearing a cap and gown was required for this graduation, it wasn't so bad for me to walk across the stage with my right arm facing the audience.

Whenever I take pictures, I mostly show my left side to the camera, and at my grade twelve graduation, my godmother called me out on it. She said, "Nika, why are you hiding your arm with the flowers? And why are you taking all your pictures just on your left side and neglecting your right?" I was speechless at first, but then I responded with a CYA (Cover Your Ass) excuse by saying, "It's just my good side. Everyone has their good side when taking pictures." My mother was giving me the eye, and I definitely knew the reason, so I took pictures on my right side too, while letting out the biggest sigh. I know it's the right thing to do. Everyone on my Facebook page knows me quite well and knows I have a physical disability. But I am still battling my crushed self-esteem. I began to post pictures showing my right arm because this lady was the first one outside of my family and best friends to call me out on hiding my disability. It was a wakeup call for me. I cannot continue to hide this part of me and be embarrassed. If I can't even accept myself, how can I expect others to do so?

Sometimes I'm embarrassed to go to the gym, because people stare at my arm. I often go to workout and do some aerobics when no one is in the room, and if someone comes in, I'll quickly finish up what I was doing and go back out to do something else. I hate running on a treadmill because of the way I have to hold my arm up on the side of my body using the full strength of my right shoulder and the side of my neck to support it, which causes pain that I feel not only during my workout but also after. If I don't hold it, it swings back and forth, which is annoying and looks odd. Sure, getting an arm sling sounds like a wise idea, but I truly dislike the increased attention I get when I wear one.

There were times when I hated looking at myself in the mirror but I would force myself to and learned to embrace my beauty and love myself. It is still a struggle, especially when I wake up every day and check out myself in the mirror. I'm always noticing some flaw in myself, but I combat the negatives by focusing on the things I love about myself, like my eyes, my curves, and my beautiful smile.

I'm always catching people, both older and younger, sometimes taking pictures and videos of my arm. One time I lost my cool and told two young women off for doing it, although it makes me angry and anxious to say anything. It's so easy for people to silently take pictures of any little thing nowadays and quickly post it for the world to see. I was also with my younger sister and she was also upset at what they were doing. I don't believe I set a good example as an older sister by speaking to them in such a way, regardless if they were in the wrong. I now see that they're only giving me more to speak about when it comes to discussing resilience and perseverance, being humble, and keeping my composure as I mature and find better ways of dealing with such situations.

Store employees follow me sometimes, because I'm constantly taking my right arm in and out of my right jacket or sweater pocket. I assume they think I'm stealing, but they sure look dumbfounded when I take my arm out to show them, and they immediately start apologizing. I usually respond with, "You can keep your sorry, because that's all you'll ever be."

I find myself struggling with weight loss. When I'm motivated, I definitely put in the work and see the results and the difference in my fitness level. The only problem is staying committed to clean eating, physical fitness and other areas of self-care, like my mental health. I find that the main reasons why I fall off and stop keeping up with a regimen is my excuses—not enough time because of work or school or helping to take care of the family, being overwhelmingly tired, mentally drained, depressed, overstressed, or dealing with anxiety. I can't continue like this and I've been working on not letting history repeat itself. I saw what happened to my Mom where she was so fixated on making sure her family was good, she neglected her own physical, mental, emotional, and spiritual well-being. Her health began to deteriorate, and now she is no longer here. The big message that I learned from her example is to put self-care first. I've heard it at school and people speak about it in the workplace too. You can burn out and even have an emotional breakdown. I wish I could've done more to help her, but all I can do is take it as a life lesson, and take care of myself first, always.

CHAPTER 11

What Will My Future Hold?

I would love to have children in the future, after marriage. I worry a lot about what will happen to me during pregnancy, and what will happen when it comes to taking care of my baby by myself without the use of both arms. How will I support their head? How will I hold the baby and multitask to get something prepared for them? How will I hold them to bathe them? How will I take the baby out of the crib, cradle, or playpen? My husband, other family members and support workers may have to assist me all the time, with almost everything. My independence will be limited when it comes to my infant. One of the best parts is that I get to rest more, but I worry that I will become annoying after needing to ask for help so much. I even worry about the delivery. I am scared that my pelvic bone is as small as my mother's, and I won't be able to have natural birth. I am afraid I will need a Caesarian section every time. Sometimes I even worry if my children will be taunted because of my disability.

I've recently learned about safe assistive devices that can help me to be more independent including some that help with taking care of an infant, or steering a car. Others such as custom cribs and cradles, car seats that swivel, special feeding high chairs, and slings to help keep my arm in place when doing physical activities are incredibly helpful! I am really glad that I came to learn about these assistive devices now instead of later when I actually have children. I recently searched Brachial Plexus Injury (BPI) on Facebook and came across a few support groups that had hundreds of people of all ages with BPI. Some acquired BPI after an accident while others acquired their injury at birth. They would speak to their experiences, ask questions, share stories and updates on their recoveries as well as provide information about assistive devices, or programs and services they utilize to help them with their injury. I wish my parents had this kind of support when I was younger. They should've been able to talk to other parents going through the same thing. Not having the programs or support services taught them so much and made them stronger for having to go through it by themselves.

When my sister was a toddler, I used to get into trouble for trying to lift her out of her crib and stroller. Even though I was always careful, I still got in trouble because I could have dropped her due to not having the support of two hands to lift her carefully. I felt horrible and embarrassed but Mom would remind me that it wasn't my fault. It was for my safety and the safety of the baby. I never really trusted myself to hold babies after that, unless I'm sitting down and someone brings me the baby.

In May 2014, I was certified as a community basketball coach, and I wanted to coach basketball within my community. However, certain basic fundamentals, like chest passing, crossovers, cross dribbling, and moving the ball in a circular motion around my body, weaving in and out between my legs and above my head, are nearly impossible for me to do, because you must use two hands. I can definitely teach these skills, but when it comes to demonstrations, I need to have someone there who knows the drills and is willing to just listen to what I say and demonstrate the moves for me. It saddens me that I can't do it independently. Once, during a training session, I left and went to the bathroom, because I got so emotional due to the fact that all the instructions required both hands or just my right hand and it was too fast for me to find accommodations for myself. My boyfriend was there and came to find me. I didn't start crying until I got to the bathroom. When I got out, he was there waiting at the door. He told me afterwards that he knew I was upset because of the drills we were instructed to do that I couldn't do. He told me he was watching me and noticed that I was getting upset, but still saw that I was trying, and then when he turned his back, I was gone. Not being able to do things like everyone else in a crowd can still hurt my feelings.

I cry sometimes while worrying about my future. I fall into depression and become extremely emotional at times, thinking of what can happen in terms of my physical and mental health. I plan on being independent and having kids. Everyday things like taking care of them or cleaning my home, will become a challenge when there isn't anyone there to assist me. After a short period of time, my back hurts and my left arm becomes fatigue from repetitive tasks but I still try not to complain. I also cannot lift anything that requires two hands without assistance. My body overcompensates on a daily basis, and it's on autopilot so much that I don't even realize how much my disabilities affect other parts of my body until I feel the pain later on. To do certain things my body will twist automatically from the left to help activate muscles to compensate for my right arm. Although during therapy I'm being trained to not activate these muscles, I've been doing this for so long that it just feels natural for me to do it. My fitness trainer and physiotherapist noticed this before I did. It explains why I have back or chest pains sometimes. I literally have to trick my brain into not allowing my body to overcompensate and cause unnecessary pain. Starting massage therapy has also helped to ease the pain and release tension in my muscles and joints.

I come up with ways to accommodate myself sometimes, and if I am doing something that requires the assistance of someone else, I try to come up with ways in which they can accommodate me. I find it interesting that though certain businesses, venues, services, programs, agencies, and public places are supposed to accommodate persons with special needs, according to the Disability Law Act, they aren't shown how. Not everyone can advocate for themselves, so I suggest that all the individuals in these places be trained on how to accommodate, instead of just being told to do it.

I have a fear of developing arthritis in my left arm and joints due to overusing my left side, as well as developing severe back pain. My doctor looked me in the face once and said, "Yes, you will eventually have arthritis, so take it easy on the tasks." It's easier said than done, but she's absolutely right. However, it's hard to take it easy. Hopefully, with therapy such as massage, physio and chiropractic therapy I can prevent it from creeping up on me for as long as I possibly can.

A couple of years ago, my parents wanted me to begin learning how to drive. They felt that I would be a great driver, so I obtained my G1 beginners license and began to practise with Dad. I was very eager to learn to drive. For months, I imagined myself behind the wheel of every car that passed me by. I knew there would be challenges, of course, but I also knew there were ways around them. When he taught me certain manoeuvres, he would keep his right arm down and figure out ways I could do them also, just like when he used to teach me how to play video games with one hand, but this was not a game, of course. Some of the manoeuvres were hard to do, especially when it came to spinning the wheel a few revolutions to the left or right, without the wheel slipping from my left hand. That's when I started to research spinner knobs, like the ones some bus drivers or old-fashioned vehicles used to assist in steering. When I first began to look around I found that the only way I could obtain one was if I went to a rehabilitation school and got assessed by an occupational therapist. The cost for that whole process was just over $500. I had already gotten assessed by an occupational therapist who had suggested I needed the spinner knob, but there was nowhere that I could purchase one.

I attended a special driving school that taught me in-car lessons using their spinner knob equipment, which was great because they are experienced in teaching drivers with disabilities. I was quite frustrated before finding this school, because no other driving school nearby catered to those with disabilities. I called about ten schools across my city, and most answers were, "I'm sorry, but we do not know how to help with that. We don't have anyone here who specializes in that." The school costs more than what the average driving school costs, but it was for my safety and learning, because until I am fully confident in myself to drive with my disability, and have mastered all the safety manoeuvres, it is still quite scary for me to drive. Since then I've obtained my G2 license and can drive on my own without a G licensed driver in the passenger seat. I plan on going back to driving school soon to get prepared for obtaining my G license so that I can drive on the freeway.

CHAPTER 12

The Sky is the Limit

On March 8, 2017, I spoke at the International Women's Day Financial Empowerment workshop, where women shared their life experiences with regards to finances, and the things they've learned to help them manage their finances. I was honoured to have been asked by one of my mentors, who organized this event, to be one of the five panelists to speak to the wonderful audience of women. I was quite nervous and I had some things written down, but when I stopped reading off my phone and just spoke from the heart, everything flowed naturally. I was a bit intimidated at first, because the panelists were mostly women who were much older than me, including elderly women, so when I spoke about my experiences I didn't want to make it seem as if I knew more than they did. I spoke about the passing of my mother and having to deal with grief, while having to take responsibility and continuing to work the week after. I spoke about how many responsibilities I carry, that it's a learning process, and that although my siblings are young, it is important to teach them about budgeting for needs versus wants. I shared some of the lessons I had learned from my parents growing up, such as prioritizing bills and paying them on time, saving money for a rainy day, and avoiding credit card debt.

After speaking, I met many empowering women, with whom I networked. I was intrigued and inspired by their stories. They also told me that my story of strength, perseverance, and resilience inspired them and moved some of them to tears. Some ladies shared their survival stories with me, especially the elderly ladies. Growing up, I didn't really have a grandmother figure in my life after my great-grandmother passed away in 2005, so when these ladies approached me with their stories and the lessons they had learned, and prayed with me, wished me well, and gave me big hugs, while smiling and laughing, it was a great feeling. I felt as if they were my grandmothers for a brief moment, which was very comforting.

I am a person who loves to take on every opportunity that comes my way, meet new people, and experience new adventures. I find that it is also hard for me to say "No", even when I'm overwhelmed, out of fear of missing out on an amazing experience. My mentors are always inviting me to participate in events. I am either speaking by myself or within a group, singing for the event, or sharing a random spoken word piece. I'm not sure why, but I usually doubt myself before I do anything, with my heart beating out of my chest, but I always end up doing well. I am so grateful for the wonderful and supportive people I have around me. Opportunities like these allow me to break out of my shell, and expose me to a whole new network of people each time.

In September 2016, I became a Youth Amplifier at the Office of the Provincial Advocate for Children and Youth. Staff of the Office advocate for children and youth who are in care in Ontario. Within the Office, there are several projects that represent a diverse selection of children and youth in Ontario, such as First Nations youth, youth who have special needs, young people in the child welfare system, youth receiving mental health services, and adolescents involved with the justice system. I was hired specifically to work with the "We Have Something to Say" project, which shines a light on children and youth across Ontario with special needs. The project helps share their stories and lived experiences to ensure that the services and programs provided to them are meeting their needs. They also share recommendations made by young people concerning how these programs and services can be improved. I had the opportunity to meet many youth and help amplify their voices to ensure that their stories, questions, and concerns were being heard by government and addressed by key stakeholders and decision makers on a systemic level.

As a Youth Amplifier, I was responsible for: co-leading, planning and facilitating community projects, public speaking events, outreach, youth engagement, social media management, and research.

Before I became a Youth Amplifier, I was already involved with the "We Have Something to Say" project. I had made a submission describing my experiences and idea for change for inclusion in the report, *We Have Something to Say*, that was released on May 10th, 2016. At that time, I was one of the volunteer Youth Advisors who helped drive the project. I was asked by project leaders, a few weeks before the launch, to speak at the "listening table" at the conference. Many stakeholders and government decision-makers were there to listen to youth like me who volunteered to bravely share our stories. I was very intimidated and nervous, because we, the youth, were scattered around the table and sat right next to these people. I was the last one to speak, and there were about twenty of us. When it was time for me to give my presentation, I could feel all the eyes in the room on me. I was glad I was given the platform to speak, and took the opportunity to present the following speech:

> *"Because it is very hard for anyone, especially youth nowadays, to obtain employment, I send off resumes, do job searches, and network with agencies as if it is my quarter-time job. There are jobs out there that I just cannot do and apply for, because they require both hands. There still aren't enough jobs out there for everyone, and as a young graduate, most employers are looking for people with years of experience. So when any job opportunity comes my way, I jump on it, regardless of the type of job it is. I have even tried youth agencies that cater to those with disabilities, such as YES: Youth Employment Services and Tropicana Youth Services, and even with those wonderful resources, employment is still*

hard to obtain.

As someone with a physical disability, it is my responsibility and human right to let my hiring managers know of my disability and the accommodations I will need while on the job. However, I still feel as if I'm a burden and a bother if I ask for accommodations, such as an extra break from sitting or standing too long due to my scoliosis, or not doing certain tasks because I may injure myself by using one hand. The reason I feel this way is because when employers are putting out the posting for the job they are hiring for, I don't believe one of their priorities in that moment is to prepare to make changes for someone like me, until after the interview when I bring it up and then they have to make the accommodations. I fear that because I bring it up during the interview, it is the reason why sometimes I do not get a call back for the job. I end up hiding my disability until after I get the job, because I fear that if I disclose it too early, they may give someone else the job to save them the trouble of making the accommodations for me.

My resume and cover letter have gotten professional tweaking, and I've done mock interviews at school, with friends and family, to prepare for actual interviews, just to ensure I do my very best. So in a way, I believe that I am being judged based on my disability rather than on my abilities. I currently work at a movie theatre at the concession, and even though they are aware of my disability, I just remain humble with my job and the tasks assigned, and work twice as hard with one arm to prove that I am just as capable as any other employee in there. I always ensure my customer service is on point, and I keep a smile on my face at all times.

I have to mentally prepare myself for every shift,

whether to face a discriminative guest or to get injured. I've gotten injured many times at work, and I feel like I am an inconvenience. When I dropped something heavy on my foot because I couldn't reach out and grab it with my other hand, fifty percent of the reason why I was crying was because I was blaming myself for having a disability, feeling as if I shouldn't be working there at all. I sat at the hospital most of the time wondering whether or not I should quit this job due to my disability and my safety, but I didn't do it, because I knew I needed to work.

I have served many guests, at least one every shift, who look at my arm rudely, and I've even caught them whispering, looking disgusted, or laughing after noticing my arm, as if I shouldn't be serving food while having a physical disability, and that hurts and is depressing. One guest had the audacity to talk aloud to his friend, as if I weren't there, about how upset he was that I was handling his food. In order to avoid these situations, I have to pivot to my right and then turn back to my left to grab the food behind me, hiding my arm in order to prevent the guest from seeing it. Not only do I have to remember my script from work when serving a guest, but I have to remind myself like, "Okay, remember to pivot, provide extra customer service beyond my disability, and smile regardless of their reaction. Don't get upset if they become rude about it."

My workplace cannot control these guests, so I remain humble and remember that these are the challenges I have, are currently facing, and will continue to face, until there is more done to raise awareness and educate people more about accommodations that need to be made for the equal treatment of youth with disabilities, like me, who are trying their hardest to fairly blend into society and be considered "normal" enough not to be judged for having a physical disability.

I would like to thank you for taking the time to listen to my story. Enjoy the rest of your day".

After my speech, many people approached me and told me how much my story inspired them and how well-spoken I was in delivering my heartfelt message to the audience. I walked up to other youth whom I hadn't met before who had also spoken, and told them how much their stories inspired me as well. One of my friends who was also on the Youth Advisory for the conference told me about the Youth Amplifier position. I was dreading the collections agency job I had just started at the time. I had to go above and beyond my limits to prove I needed the job, and it took a huge toll on me. I had only been there for a month prior to the conference. I saw how annoyed they got when I told them that my left hand and wrist became very sore while typing, because it was a constant test of typing speed and was very repetitive. When I couldn't go fast enough for them, they'd get agitated, but I had to remind them about my disability. I didn't belong there at all. It was way too much to sit there for eight hours, killing myself to keep up typing with one hand before I lost calls. That was bad for business, and I remember losing a lot of their calls because I was getting backed up. Not only that, but I was dealing with difficult people yelling in my ear and cursing at me. I just felt like I was becoming a burden when I started to ask for accommodation, so I cut myself loose.

I ended up picking up a summer job as a camp coordinator. I loved the camp, and it was a great thing to keep me busy during the summer. But I needed a full-time, all-around job, and I was already worried about what I would do after the camp was done in August. Luckily, late in August I received a call from the Advocate's Office informing me I had gotten the job as a Youth Amplifier. I was so excited about the position that I quit the camp a little early so that I could start the Youth Amplifier job on time.

I believe it was my calling, because I loved everything about the work. Being a leader, advocating for positive change, and showing others how to advocate for themselves, constantly networking with others, volunteering, travelling, attending conferences and events, speaking to others and inspiring them with my story and my experiences. For as long as I can remember, I have been told that I am a leader, an advocate for positive change, and a positive example to others, so when I obtained this position, I felt at home. The only unfortunate thing was that the position only lasted one year. However, within the year I got to practice my public speaking skills, enhancing the skills I had, met a bunch of amazing individuals, liaised and networked with other organizations, travelled outside of Toronto to conduct outreach on behalf of the Advocate's Office and, most importantly, was part of creating change. Doing this has shown me exactly where I need to be career-wise, effortlessly doing what I love and being paid, while not having to worry whether I'm putting myself at risk of injury due to my disability. Taking on these volunteer and networking opportunities opened doors for even more opportunities for me to better myself and do what I love to do.

I found that writing a memoir helped me to revisit many of the negative things that occurred in my life that I had buried deep within and refused to deal with for a very long time. Doing so sometimes caused waves of sadness, anger, and depression. There were times when I needed a mental break, and stopped writing for weeks. I am grateful that most days my drive and dedication helped me overcome the feelings that prevented me from writing. Sitting down for too long hurt my back some days, so I'd lay down flat on my stomach and type. I'd then begin lying on my right arm, because in a weird way it's most comfortable, until about fifteen minutes later when I'd feel my arm start to cramp and go numb. I'd stop to sit up for a few seconds, but then get right back to it shortly after, because my drive, my dedication, and my need to understand "*why*" were bigger than any physical discomfort I was feeling. I'd feel the pain, but because my thoughts were flowing so much, I couldn't stop because I was afraid I would lose what I wanted to say. There were many nights I couldn't sleep because my book was on my mind. There were many mornings when as soon as I opened my eyes my book was on my mind. When you want something this bad, and you know it's bound to happen, when you have faith, when you pray, when you find the strength, when you feel it coming just for you, and when you put in the work, you will get it done.

Having a disability throughout my life did not, and will not, disable my willingness, my passion, my perseverance, my resilience, and my drive to do what I want to do in life, to love, and to keep living. All the hardship I endured, and all the love and support I had, and will continue to have, has helped to shape me into the person I am today. It has taught me many valuable life lessons. When people meet me, they always think I am much older than I am, not because of the way I look, but because of the way I carry myself with confidence and maturity. I am twenty-two years old and have gone through a lot, but I am encouraged by the fact that I am lucky and I still have a chance every day to get up and to try again.

A lot of people have judged me and mocked my disability, thinking that it was going to stop me. They thought that it was going to forever prevent me from reaching the places and heights I wanted to reach in life. Those same people made me hate myself. I still encounter these ill-informed individuals, every now and then, who laugh and stare. I still catch people sometimes, especially on public transit, who pull their smart phones out and start videoing me. Sounds ridiculous, right? I've seen it, and my friends who are with me have seen it too. I've confronted many of those people. Sometimes I'm yelling and screaming while cursing them out for having the audacity to stoop so low. I got so far up into one lady's personal space, that I accidently poked my index finger right into her face. They have no idea what I go through on a daily basis to mentally prepare myself to face people like them, and keep my cool by letting go and just walking away. My anxiety worsens when going through public spaces, because I'm worried that someone may be recording my exposed right arm and sharing it for laughs. Sometimes it's so bad I feel a wave of paranoia come over me when I notice someone's phone is up directly facing my right side when my arm isn't hidden and tucked away in my right jacket pocket. Summer is the worst time of year for this, because I wear sleeveless clothing more often and I get even more stares.

Recently, I had a conversation with one of my best friends, Bree, and she said that I can't always get angry when I notice people doing this. I have to realize that it isn't me who has the problem, it's them. How can they live in a society where it's the norm to accept people with disabilities, then turn around and make fun of us when they notice it? It's hard enough to constantly need to make changes to accommodate ourselves to try and normalize our daily lives, without having ignorant people like them making it even more challenging for us.

Bullies made me hate the gift that God gave me to work with, but their taunts also helped me find strength. I am certain that if the shoe was on the other foot, many of those who judge and mock people with disabilities would not be able to cope. I believe the Lord gives his toughest battles to his toughest soldiers and gives no one more than they can handle. I have been fighting my entire life, seeking accommodation after accommodation, suppressing my emotions in situations to be the "bigger" person all the while I'm being laughed at or recorded or being made to feel that I should hold myself back from opportunities simply because I have a disability. Even in my darkest moments I have found the inner strength to hold myself back from committing suicide, because I know I'm surrounded by many people who love, admire, care about and support me.

I am very thankful for the lessons I was taught by my parents about life. I am so glad that I was blessed to have such parents. Sure, they both grew up without their own parents in their lives and didn't have much, but their turnaround was to be better parents for their own children, no matter what. They tried their hardest to give me and my siblings what they didn't have growing up. They were raised by other family members and by "their village"—like the old saying, "It takes a village to raise a child"—who made them the amazing parents they became. Our mother passed away at only forty years of age, but because of her and our father we know love, we know humility, we know happiness, we know togetherness, and we are truly grateful. I will continue to pass that on to my younger siblings and godchildren, and eventually my own children and nieces and nephews when the time comes.

I would like to leave you, dear reader, with this thought: yes, I have a physical disability, but one thing I know for sure is that doctor who caused my injury at birth did not take away my intelligence, resilience, and determination to live a full rich life. He ripped some major nerves from my spinal cord, an injury that can never be mended by surgery, physiotherapy or any form of treatment and I may have gone through excruciating pain before taking my very first breath, but I am here now. I was always a very bright and inquisitive child from the very beginning. I've been through way too much for me to let those who wish to make me feel bad about myself win. This consistent fight to get through every dark night guarantees that there'll always be more chances to make things right in the brighter days ahead, like Momma said.

Many times, in the midst of feeling self-hatred, I feel extreme hatred towards the doctor who delivered me. I realize that hate is a strong word, and I don't truly hate him. I just wonder why this had to happen to me; out of all the babies he delivers every day, why me? I had to change my mentality and think of it like this: *I was the chosen one. I was the one chosen to fight this particular battle alongside the Lord, and turn it around into something positive. I was the one who was the strongest to fight this battle. So, I can either sit and complain or use my experiences to grow as a person and for a higher purpose.*

I believe that forgiveness is the key to finding inner peace. However, I wish my birth doctor had been more concerned about the best interest of his patients and conducted a C-section procedure on my mother. I wish he had an emergency C-section room set up. I wish he hadn't panicked and started yanking my head. I wish he had called for help. I wish he had referred my mother to the hospital where she wanted to have me, even if he didn't know anyone there. It would've taken just one phone call to get the information he needed. Time may have been a factor, but the call would've at least shown my parents that he was trying to put their wishes for their child and their best interests first. I wish he hadn't told my mother the injury was her fault for being "full-figured," which is ridiculous, and took responsibility for his actions as a medical practitioner. I wish he hadn't given my parents false hope by telling them my injury would disappear in two days. They desperately waited two days...two weeks... two months and then two years with no improvement in my situation. It's twenty-two years later and my Brachial Plexus Birth Injury hasn't gotten any better.

However, with tears running down my face, I forgive this human being. He is human. For my inner peace and sanity, I have learned to do this. I've hated him throughout my entire life for all the bad things my physical disability has caused me. Sure, he could've done better in the way he went about his procedures and the way he spoke to my parents, but I still forgive him. And you know what? In a way, I thank him too. If I hadn't endured that birth injury I wouldn't have been the extremely strong, perseverant, resilient, adaptable person I am today. My parents are all these things and more, because it was they, on their own, who taught me how to cope with dealing with society and how to adapt. There are many others who have had a major effect on my life who helped shape the person I am today. The experiences, all I had to go through because of my disability, revealed the better version of me. There will be future struggles, trials, and hardships, but there will also be triumphs, rewarding experiences, and blessings as a result of everything I've gone through. I'm going to continue to hold on to that faith, and pray. I have comfort in knowing that "after every dark night, there's a brighter day ahead." My mother always said that no matter what you go through, there's always a light at the end of the tunnel where things will begin to get better.

I have forgiven the doctor who did this to me, and so should everyone else. Everyone makes mistakes, and yes, this was a major one, but did that stop me? No. Is he a bad guy? No. Should he have listened to my mother's initial wishes? Yes, he should have. But in some way, not listening to her turned out for the best.

Many people wonder how I remain so strong, and why. Had it not been for my enduring faith, I would not have been in the position that I am today. There are many times when I'd sit and ask myself, "How did I make it through all this? How did I bear everything and push through?"

It's "Footprints" I tell you. This poem speaks to my life so much. A picture of the same poem has been in my home for as long as I can remember, even after moving homes several times. It wasn't until after my mother passed away that I truly began to understand the meaning behind the poem and how it resonates in my life. I grew to learn that the Lord has carried me through great trials and triumphs. I did not walk alone. Thank the Lord for giving me the guidance and strength to push through and continue writing this book even after Mommy passed away. He has helped me to continue forward, to persevere, and to remain resilient through prayer, hope, and faith. Everything I've ever been through, from the injury that I endured at birth, to my childhood, to being a teenager, even now as a young adult, I have never been alone and I've made it here today.

DEAR FAMILY AND FRIENDS

My "why" is my immediate family: my mother, father, younger sister, and younger brother. They are the ones who strengthen me and keep me focused through everything. Everything I do, they are right there in my mind, filtering my actions. They are my number-one fans and number-one supporters. My love, and their love, is everlasting and unconditional. I love you all so much.

About a year after my mother passed away, we came across a nine-page handwritten letter, that was dated and signed by her. She was explaining what had happened to me at birth, how she felt about it, how I was doing at eight years old, and what her worries were for my future.

Wynnikka Matthews
Delivery & Recovery.

My water broke on October 11/95, around noon. I called he told me to go over to the hospital ( ). I checked in and I didn't start having active labour until 7:30 AM Oct/12/95. months ~~before~~ going into the hospital, I had asked the Dr. if I could have a C-section he ask why, he also informed me that it wouldn't be in my best interest to have that done, because I could die on the operating table. At this point I started to ask about referring me to

another doctor & he got pissed
off. because he snapped at me.
by saying that he doesn't know
of any doctors @
where I had requested to deliver.
He told me that this was my
first baby so I basically don't
know what I'm talking about.
I was refered to . by
a very good Dr. I had him
from the age of six. until now.
his name is . I
was 9cm dialated when .
said that I can start to
push if I feel the urge to.
I had a hard time pushing
Wynnikka's head was out but

Pg 3

her shoulders were stuck, the Dr. was pulling & pulling on her head & using forecepts until he decided to have the nurse push on my belly to help the baby out. When Wynnikka was finally delivered, she was non responsive. She didn't cry, she didn't move. He put the baby down on my chest for about a minute, then he put her under this light that he said would warm her up. They took me to my room & took the baby else where for awhile. I had no idea what was going on, they just told me

pg 4

not to worry. When the baby
came back il notice she had
a little hat on, when il tried
to take it off. & she would
let out a little cry, so il left
it alone. The next day the
doctor came to see me, the
first thing he said to me was
that the baby's arms are
going to start moving properly
in two days. He also said
that this was my fault why
this was happening to my
baby due to the fact that
il was full figured. He made
me feel guilty right there on
the spot, not knowing at the

pg 5

time that he was full of it. He just wanted to clear himself from all responsibility. I would like to say for the record that I'm still full figured, since Wynnikka, I had a healthy bouncing baby boy, who is now five years old & I just gave birth to a healthy baby girl on & I had her by C-Section. so he is really full of it. I'm still angry but I try not to show it. He lied to me, "big time" not to mentioned he made me feel guilty over something I had no control over. Wynnikka is a very bright & capable little

9.6

girl. She is a A&B Student.
She's very smart, she does everything
possible that anyone else can
do. Wynnikka sometimes has to
deal w/ social skills due to some
Kids teasing about her arm &
she has to always explain her
situation or justify why it is
that she may take a little longer
to do normal everyday things
or why she does it in her own
way. I don't put any physical
limitations on Wynnikka, What ever
she wants to attempt to do, I let
her as long as she's not going
hurt herself or anyone else.
She rode a two Wheeler @ age four

pg 7

& some kids w/o any disability can't. Wynnikka has a lot of questions as to why this had to happen to her. I believe that one day soon Wynnikka will get what she deserves from this doctor, who has robbed her of her ability to function like any ordinary person w/ two working arms & hands. Wynnikka has a lot of courage to try & do everything possible, She has a lot of support & gets a lot of encouragements from her Dad & I. We have been through a lot & still going through it. Wynnikka's arm cramps up & hurts, this is when our hearts pain to see this happening to her. We can only pg. 8

imagine what she's really going through. Wynnikka needs to be compensated so that she can attend all sorts of programs that can help her out physically, emotionally & mentally. I put her in activities outside of school but perhaps it's not enough. Doctor & his insurance company should pay the cost for this, not to mention she should have a trust fund set up so she has a well & secure future without any worries of discrimination trying to obtain a job. Right after Wynnikka was born the placenta went up in the air & fell on his head &

pg. 9

On his body. He got a little upset & asked me if I had anything acute wrong w/me. I said then & still think it, was a sign from the Creator that he had done something very wrong. He mentioned to me also that it had never ever happened to him before. The moral of this story is that my daughter has a disability due to the fact that Dr. wasn't patient enough to wait & deliver my baby girl properly.

[signature] Pearce Dec 5th 2003

I appreciate this letter she wrote because her side of the story still lives on forever, even after her passing away. It was a blessing to have stumbled upon it before completing my book so that she, as the mother of a child with a special need, can still be heard although she is no longer here to speak on it. Being able to read her account of what happened in vivid detail is a blessing even though she had told me the story many times throughout my life.

Below is the transcribed version of my mother's handwritten letter.

Wynnikka Matthews
Delivery & Recovery

My water broke on Oct/11/95, around noon. I called the doctor and he told me to go over to the hospital. I checked in and I didn't start having active labour until 7:30 am Oct/12/95. Months before going to the hospital, I had asked the doctor if I could have a C-section. He asked why, then he also informed me that it wouldn't be in my best interest to have that done, because I could die on the (operating) table. At this point, I started to ask about referring me to another doctor and he got pissed off because he snapped at me by saying that he didn't know of any doctor at the hospital where I wanted to be referred to and had previously requested to deliver.

He told me this was my first baby so I basically don't know what I was talking about. I was referred to him by my very good family doctor at the time that I had from the age of six until now. I was 9cm dilated when the doctor told me to start to push if I felt the urge to. I had a hard time pushing. Wynnikka's head was out but her shoulders were stuck, the doctor was pulling and pulling on her head and using forceps until he decided to have the nurse push on my belly to help the baby out. When Wynnikka was finally delivered, she was non-responsive. She didn't cry, she didn't move. He put the baby down on my chest for a minute, then he put her under this light, that he said would warm her up. They took me to my room and took her elsewhere for a while. I had no idea what was going on; they just told me not to worry. When the baby came back, I noticed she had a little hat on; when I tried to take it off, she would let out a little cry, so I left it alone.

The next day, the doctor came to see me, and the first thing he said to me was that the baby's hands were going to start moving properly in two days. He also said that this was my fault why this was happening to my baby, due to the fact that I was full-figured. He made me feel guilty right there on the spot, not knowing at the time that he was full of it. He just wanted to clear himself from all responsibility.

I would like to say that for the record, I am still full-figured. Since Wynnikka, I had a healthy, bouncing baby boy, who is now five years old and I just gave birth to a healthy baby girl by C-section, so he was really full of it. I'm still angry, but I try not to show it. He lied to me, BIG TIME, not to mention, he made me feel guilty over something I had no control over.

Wynnikka is a very bright and capable little girl. She is an A and B student. She is very smart; she does everything possible that anyone else can do. Wynnikka sometimes has to deal with social skills due to some kids teasing her about her arm and she always has to explain her situation or justify why it is that she may take a little longer to do normal, everyday things or why she does it in her own way. I don't put any physical limitations on Wynnikka; whatever she wants to attempt to do, I let her do, as long as she's not going to hurt herself or anyone else.

She rode a "two-wheeler" (bicycle) at the age of four, and some kids without any disability can't. Wynnikka has a lot of questions as to why this had to happen to her. I believe one day soon Wynnikka will get what she deserves from the doctor who has robbed her of her ability to function like an ordinary person with two working arms and hands. Wynnikka has a lot of courage to try and do everything possible.

She has a lot of support from her dad and I. We have been through a lot and are still going through it. Wynnikka's arm cramps up and hurts, this is when our hearts pain to see this happening to her. We can only imagine what she's really going through. Wynnikka needs to be compensated so that she can attend all sorts of programs that can help her out physically, emotionally, and mentally. I put her in activities outside school, but perhaps it's not enough. The doctor and his insurance company should pay the cost for this. Not to mention, she should have a trust fund set up so she has a well and secure future without any worries of discrimination trying to obtain a job.

Right after Wynnikka was born, the placenta went up in the air and fell on his head, then on his body. He got a little upset, and asked me if I had anything acute wrong with me (diseases). I said no then, and I still think it was a sign from the Creator that he had done something wrong. He mentioned to me also that it had never happened to him before.

The moral if this story is that my daughter has a disability due to the fact that the doctor wasn't patient enough to wait and deliver my baby girl properly.

Signed & Dated – Nicole Pearce
Dec 5th 2003

A note from my father, Winston:

*I have been hurt since the day she was born, because we had a perfectly healthy baby, and then this happened. Every day her mother and I prayed for a miracle after the doctor said that the condition would go away on its own. Because he used silver spoon things (*forceps*) to pull her out and because she had spots (*lacerations*) on her head, we were afraid of her having brain damage. Thank goodness, she didn't have any brain damage. As she got older, we saw the difference in her arms. At a few months, she raised her left arm for the first time, and we caught a photo of the moment. We did notice that one (the right) was smaller than the other, and she would cry for pain. At the children's hospital, before and after her surgery, we saw kids of different ages that had the same thing, and were healthy babies and were very smart. That gave us hope for Nika. We let her do everything she wanted, but disciplined her like any other ordinary child. We let her make her own mistakes and get into trouble to learn her lessons, as long as she wasn't hurting herself or anyone else. We taught her how to do things in special ways to help her with her independence when we weren't around to help her, things like personal hygiene, buttoning buttons, zipping zippers using her mouth to assist, and putting on a jacket or hat (right arm in first then left). She is a very bright child who cried in early elementary school if she got anything less than an A+. We wanted to make sure she did her very best in school and got great grades, because we knew it would happen. We were scared for when she started grade school; we were worried that she would be teased, judged, and bullied by others for her disability. She did so well and her teachers loved her. From grade one, almost every single day she came home with a story of how another kid pushed her around, called her retarded, took her stuff away,* *mocked her clapping, isolated her, called her stupid, got mad at her because she was put on someone's team by the teacher when no one wanted her on their team, laughed at the way she did something physically, didn't eat with her at lunch, and more. There is so much, so much. I used to sit there and cry with her and Nicole about how bad we felt and how much she needs to keep fighting in a good way and forgive them. Teachers gave her D's and R's because she couldn't physically do something. I ran outside one day in my pajamas to yell at a bunch of kids who followed her home after school and took her backpack and threw it in dog shit, put it on a pole where she couldn't reach it, and called her a retarded bitch. The school superintendent was called, and there were meetings to discuss the bullying many times. She went to different middle schools to avoid the bullying, but it started every single time, and it hurt us. She came home and took it out on her younger siblings by yelling at them and ignoring them when she got home.*

She still worked hard in school and got great grades. And it got better as she got older. We are so proud that she graduated from high school with honours and eight awards plus scholarships, and graduated from college straight after.

Now she is in school again and tried to work in the summer. She has a part-time job at a movie theatre, but I hate it when she works, because I worry every time that she'll hurt herself, and she does end up doing so. She hurt herself by trying to prove that she can do everything else a "normal" person like me can do. She doesn't like to sit around and mope in her disability; she loves to be active and do things to help others. She loves to talk to people, but sometimes she comes home from work upset at how people look at her in disgust when they notice her disability when taking their orders. She is insecure, but wants to be independent, and I'm scared for her future. She shouldn't have to work. I hate seeing her work, but she doesn't like to take money from me either. She hates coming forward to ask for help even now, because she is embarrassed, and feels bad. But she is my daughter, and I don't mind giving her money, but she is ashamed of her disability, even when told she should embrace it because it helped her to be who she is today. I tell her she is not allowed to cut cans, cut with a knife, lift or move anything heavy that requires two hands.

She comes home almost every day complaining about shoulder, neck, back, and joint pains. She stands for hours at a time at work, and I hate that. Because she wants to make more money, and it is only minimum wage, she will work extra each week and take others' shifts. Although she fully qualified and applied for other jobs, it's hard for her to get one because finding jobs nowadays is not easy, especially for those with disabilities.

Sometimes I have to rub her shoulders when she is pain. She got absolutely no treatment, because it is so hard to afford, especially when you have two other children. The bed she is on should be therapeutic. I worry about things like these, and it hurts my heart that I have to see her go through this, especially now without her mom around to help her with more personal things, like putting her hair up, fixing her bra, and so forth. She will always call her younger sister, her godmother, or her friends to come over and help. I even clean up her room without her asking or knowing, because sometimes it can be too much, and I see how exhausted she is sometimes. She wants to do everything and be independent, but she needs help, and she will need all the help she can get, physically and mentally, because I don't want her to get hurt in the long run. What about when she has kids? I worry so much, although she has a great head on her shoulders.

Dear Mommy & Daddy,

You two are truly my right hand, thank you, thank you, thank you. I know, Mommy, that you won't be able to read this now, but I am so grateful to have parents like you. I can only imagine as parents what you had to go through, not only physically but mentally, in order to make the best possible decisions to raise me right. Thank you for loving us unconditionally. Thank you for the affection you consistently and equally gave me, Quan, and Keys. Thank you for allowing me to be free to be myself, as long as I didn't hurt myself or anyone else. Thank you for always showing me the importance of resilience and perseverance. Thank you for reminding me every day of how beautiful I am, and that I have a bright future ahead of me. Thank you for pushing me to do well in school to prove I am more than just my disability. Thank you for putting me in programs outside of school so I felt a sense of belonging in a group. Thank you for always finding different ways of showing me how to combat the bullying I endured throughout elementary school. Thank you for the sleepless nights you spent crying after putting me back to bed, because I'd wake up in pain and you'd massage my arm or back. Thank you for always jumping to my defense. Thank you for teaching me physical, emotional, spiritual, and social self-defence. Thank you for not allowing me to fall through the cracks of the educational system. Thank you for going above and beyond the schools, and their trustees and superintendents, when things didn't work out in my best interest at school. Thank you for showing me the importance of showing people my personality first and who I am to prove to people that I am more than just my disability. Thank you for showing me the importance of taking up opportunities and meeting new people who are like-minded. Thank you for showing me the many different ways to accommodate myself and how to show others how to accommodate me when they didn't know how.

Thank you for helping me understand that when people ask me about my disability, I should not become defensive, because they are just showing their concern. And thank you for teaching me how to answer and explain it to them in the politest way possible.

Thank you and more. I love you and more. Mommy, I wish I could give you a big hug and kiss, but you are looking down now from a better place, at peace, and I know you are very proud. Everyone says it to me too, so I more than just believe it, I can feel it. Thank you for all you two have done for me, above and beyond, and for always being there. Daddy, the greatest man in my life, thank you for always being there for me. Mom used to always say how jealous she was of us, because she believed I was more of a daddy's girl. But I obviously love you both the same, like how you love all your children the same. Mommy, you put all your trust in this doctor after losing a baby prior to me, and then this happened, after knowing you had a baby that was entirely healthy before delivery. I can only imagine how you felt, and because no one really knew about this birth injury at the time, it was really hard to seek the help you and Dad needed to support me. You went through this with minimum to no support. You leaned on some friends and family members in times of need, but to raise a child with a disability requires even more support. There were no easily accessible mental, emotional, or physical help to you as parents, aside from just taking care of me. What about you? How did you do it? You, as parents, required support too to help you cope, and you pushed through without it. I salute you both for it.

When I began to go to school and got bullied for something I couldn't control, it was even harder on you guys, because I wasn't in your care during those six hours a day at school, so there was only so much protection I could get while at school. You moved me to many different elementary schools to try and protect me from the bullies or the bad-marking teachers, but each time there was a new set of kids who reminded me of the last group of bullies from the previous schools. With your love and support, my confidence was reconstructed as I grew older and I began to combat the bullying in smart ways. I can say thank you a gazillion times for all you have done and what you had to go through to raise a child with Obstetrical Brachial Plexus Injury. For all the hardship, something good will come out of it. My birth injury did not occur in vain. I am an ambassador for BPI, making it known through this story, speaking about it, and raising awareness.

Thank you for the little things. Thank you for the really big things. I love you two very much. No words can explain the amount of gratitude I feel towards you in appreciation of all you have done and all you've gone through.

Oh, and thank you for my younger brother and sister. Having them to boss around and help raise has helped to give me some of the skills it takes to be a positive advocate and role model.

Thank you!

A note from my younger brother Quan:

Growing up in the area we live in, I've seen a lot of things. One of the things I've seen that makes me overprotective of my older sister is her getting bullied. When I was younger, I used to witness my older sister getting bullied on a daily basis because of her right hand. Kids around her would go out of their way to make her feel bad for not being able to play sports and other games that require two hands, but that didn't stop her; she still played no matter the disrespect she received. Kids would pretend to be her friend, and then embarrass her in front of everyone and bully me for being her brother and defending her. In grade three, I saw my mom cry, then go over to our school after my sister's grade six teacher embarrassed her in front of the whole class for not being able to do what everyone else could do and having no friends, and she even put it on her report card, then sent her home when she retaliated. Mom lost our baby brother a week after that at four months. For days, I saw my sister come home from school crying. Days like those hurt me. When she played video games with me, I would sometimes cry after seeing how she had to play, and the things she had to do to learn how to use her left hand only. She bribed people with food and candy just to leave her alone, and they would...just for that day. I cried and threw tantrums at people. A day before her birthday, a girl took her pink and purple Bratz bag with sparkles all over it and put it in dog poo then hung it on a "No dogs allowed" sign. I cried and was shadow punching in my room. My parents went and got her a new Bratz bag that was purple and pink and looked way better, along with other gifts. Seeing her graduate made me realize that she was stronger than others thought she was, and that made me cry. She graduated with very high grades and went off and completed college and went back again to school. She never once stopped despite her disability. I have to help her a lot to put her hair in a ponytail or to help her tie a scarf because she's embarrassed and frustrated sometimes of her hair when she can't do it herself. My dad, sister, and I help her roll her sleeves up, button her jacket, tie her shoes, and carry her laundry to the laundry room. I feel so bad that my dad or I will just help her clean her room, without her asking. I hate seeing her wear make-up and wigs, or try wearing heels, because we think she's pretty, but she just does it to feel better about herself, and it makes her happy.

Dear Quan,

Quaaan! My little brother. Just because you're hovering over me now doesn't mean you automatically become older than me, but you are my little-big brother. My goodness, being your older sister, looking after you, and bossing you around from when you were younger has definitely given me the upper hand in practicing to be a leader and taking control of situations. I'm sure you remember me getting in trouble with Mom and Dad for over-bossing you around all the time. I love you very much and appreciate all the times you've stepped in to defend me from bullies when we were younger. I'm sorry for all the times I came home and took out my day on you by yelling or not playing with you because I had a really bad day at school dealing with bullies. I'm sorry for letting these same bullies bully you around at the park to avoid being bullied myself. I couldn't ask for a better younger brother. Now that you're older, you totally annoy me sometimes by trying to regulate me like you're my second dad, asking me where I'm going, what time I'm coming back, who I'm with, and what I'm wearing. Hello, excuse me, sir, last time I checked I was born first. You really crack me up, but it is all out of love, and I extend great gratitude towards Mom and Dad for teaching us the importance of loving each other and looking out for one another. Thank you for being my personal assistant when it comes to doing tasks related to my disability. Although sometimes you're more than willing to help, I feel as if

I'm bothering you.

For the times you helped with chores, the times you would randomly spread my bed if I forgot in the morning, zipping up my zippers, tying my shoes, helping me with necklaces and earrings, stopping in the midst of your video games to drain the hot pot of noodles for me and continue to assist me in the kitchen, carrying my bags or baskets of laundry to the laundromat for me, and accompanying me to ensure I was okay and much more, thank you. I know that when you think of what the doctor did to me it upsets you and makes you bitter. God knew that this was something that I could make it through. Yes, my special need is a setback in some aspects of my life, but you've seen it for yourself that I try my hardest not to allow it to come in the way, and have always tried to find a way to do what I want to do in life. It is very hard, yes, but it only makes me stronger. You've witnessed it; look at me now. I can either choose to sit, mope about it, and be sad, or make something of it and show people that I am more than just my disability. I am Wynnikka. My disability is a part of me and has helped to shape who I am today. Without it, I would not be me. Without you, I would not be me either. My big helper, my little-big brother, my bodyguard, I love you! I appreciate you.

A note from my younger sister Keys:

> *I didn't like how people would make fun of my sister and mock her hand, calling her names like "retarded", "handicapped person." We went to a street festival this summer, and a teenage girl took pictures of my sister's arm with her friends on a ride, and started laughing so hard and pointing at her. She didn't notice, but I did and told her. I wanted to yell at them, and my brother and her best friend wanted to as well, but Nika said to just leave it alone. When she comes to visit my school, sometimes mean kids my age say rude things to me about her arm too. I help her to put on and take off her bra sometimes and help her to fix her belt. I help her pull her sleeves off to take off her shirt or sweater. I help her put her hair in a ponytail. I help clean her room, and do some chores for her. She needs help a lot, and she shouldn't lift heavy things, but sometimes she doesn't listen and just wants to do it, and dad gets upset because she can hurt herself. She always needs help to carry her books or a bin or basket. She tries to do my hair for school for me like mom did, but usually gets upset because she can't do it for me, so she or my dad often pay someone else to do my hair. I don't like it when people make fun of her, because she is the nicest person and the best sister.*

Dear Keys,

Oh, Keys. Where do I begin with you? I'll start when Mom told me she was pregnant with you and didn't know your gender. She told me that if I wanted a baby sister as bad as I said, then I should pray on my knees for you, and you can bet I did. Girl, I was on my knees praying to the Lord for you almost every night, because I couldn't wait to have a baby sister and do girly things with you, like play Barbie dolls, paint your nails, and take you places. When Mom told me she was having a girl, I was super-excited to meet you. I couldn't wait. When we came to visit you at the hospital, I cried so much, and I couldn't believe I actually had a baby sister. I was just eight years old, but I wanted to help with everything, from preparing your formula, changing your diaper, to potty-training you. I potty-trained you, by the way. I helped to change your clothes, push your stroller with Mommy and Daddy. At one point, I wanted you to jump past being a toddler so you could play Barbie dolls and other games with me. I also taught you how to walk. Not even Mom or Dad believed me, until your Christening day when I made you walk down the aisle in front of everyone, and they were shocked.

Now you're much older, and I can play games with you, teach you things, and take you to places other than the park. As you became older, you became more inquisitive about things, and you began to notice things like my disability at around seven or eight years old. I remember when you asked me, and I tried to explain it in a way that you'd understand. "The doctor pulled my head and caused my arm to be this way, because he pulled nerves from my spinal cord when I got stuck in mommy's pelvic bone while I was being born. Nerves are these things that send signals from your brain to other parts of your body from your spinal cord." I don't know if you remember, but I explained this to you while visually pointing it out, then showing a picture to you of the anatomy. I don't think you understood the anatomy though. Your eight-year-old response was something like, "I hate that doctor. I don't like that he did that to you. That's bad, and he is a bad doctor. I'd hurt him back, because he hurt you." Then I said, "Oh no, Keys, don't say that. That's not nice. I know it's bad what he did to me, but don't say that, please. Look, I'm still alive and healthy. I'm still okay." Then you cutely apologized. I wanted you to know that yes, he had done that to me, but I am beyond my disability. You didn't understand it that well. All you knew was that he hurt your older sister's arm, and you hated him. I did not want you to grow up having hate towards this doctor. As you grew older, you started to be my little helper. Sometimes I feel like I'm bothering you to help me. You're a teenager now, so you help me even more with chores if Dad or Quan can't help me. You help to get me dressed with certain things I need help with, and I always appreciate your wonderful help.

Just like with Quan, I used to boss you around all the time and used to get in trouble for it if it was too much. I'm sorry for the times when we were younger and I'd take my bad days out on you, yelling and ignoring you when you wanted to play with me, or getting overly emotional over small situations by blowing them out of proportion. Quan is much older now, but after Mom passed away, when you and he were still quite young, I felt that I needed to step in and really play the role of a mother. It's been a struggle to balance being your sister while trying to raise you from a motherly perspective. Teaching you all the things Mom taught me, and instilling them within you is hard, and then having to prep you to go to high school to deal with more responsibilities, hard work, drama, bullies, and boys is hard as well. I was there about ten years ago, missy, and I can give you the advice I got from Mommy, but it is so hard knowing you'll be going through the same things. I'm such a "mother hen" Mom would say, and I'm so glad she taught me how to be that, because now that she is gone, I am the closest mother figure you have on a daily basis. Asking you how your day was every day, making sure that you are shown affection the way Mom would, spending time with you, giving you positive affirmations daily, making sure you are taking care of yourself, helping Dad to show you and Quan how to take on more responsibilities, and much more. I'm doing my best to teach you the ladylike stuff to do as a young girl, like what Mom showed me. I will continue to teach you positive self-image and self-love, and how to deal with bullies. You are the youngest one, and you are going into your tender teenage years. I can admit that this part is extremely hard, because I too am young, and I am still learning to cope with some of the same things as well. I believe this is giving me a lot of practice for when I become a mother. I will have a bit of an advantage.

Keys, thank you for being the most amazing little sister ever. Without you, I would not be me. My little helper, my bodyguard, my twin, my little partner in crime number two, I love you so much!

Dear Jaleesa & Breanna, my best friends,

You are no longer just my best friends, but are my sisters after how many years. You are so loving and supportive of me. I wouldn't ever ask for another set of best friends when I feel I have the best in the world. Thank you for always having my back. Thank you for always being there when I need you. When I feel insecure about certain things about myself, you always reassure me about how much of a "Hot Gyal" I am. You say I shouldn't allow the ignorant mindsets of others to stop me from living life how I want to, dressing how I want to and going where I want to regardless if I have a physical disability and that they'll notice. You have amazing personalities and hearts of gold. You believe in me and everything I want to achieve in life. Not only that but you've helped encourage me to get to those places and continue to push me towards my future goals. We can sit and converse for days, laughing until our abdomens hurt and we're clenching our chests, gasping for air. I cannot thank you enough and you are my best friends, here in my life to stay. My sisters, I love you so much and thank you for all you've done and continue to do. @3PlayneJanes Forever!!!

To all my other amazing friends, I love and appreciate you. Thank you for accepting me, being there for me and giving me the sense of belonging that I craved from society from I was young. Thank you for making me laugh. Thank you for allowing me to be me.

DECEMBER 3RD, 2017

This date is significant to me, and one I will never forget. This is a date that changed my life forever.

I had planned to publish this book in May 2017. Then the date changed to October 2017. All those mental breaks and procrastination periods here and there were well worth it. It's a great thing this book wasn't published earlier because on December 3rd 2017 I met my "Long Lost Sister."

I was supposed to go out to a comedy show in the evening but had gotten a last minute invitation from my friend Shakil to go to watch his friend, Truss perform. He told me that he goes to school with her and that she has a disability. He said one of her arms was similar to mine and that he wanted me to connect with her. He also told me that she sings.

I was briefly introduced to her before the show and I was already inspired. She and her friend Phoenix go by the name of "TRP.P" and they put on their first live music studio experience. It was so amazing to hear and watch them perform along with some other talented local artists. I found out that not only is Truss a singer but she is an amazing producer who makes beats! She is confident in herself and is also ridiculously hilarious!

Before the show I had already taken note of her social media handles, her website and the songs she performed that I really liked. When the event was done and everyone was mixing and mingling, I went up to Truss again to reintroduce myself to her. I told her how wonderful she and her friend Phoenix performed and thanked them for putting on such an amazing event. I told her how much she inspired me and revealed that I have Brachial Plexus Injury that occurred at birth. She then said she too has Brachial Plexus Birth Injury and we both stood there staring at each other in shock.

I took off my jacket so quick to show her my right arm and for the first time in my life I never second guessed what anyone else around me thought about my disability. I never cared. I felt free to be me. I said, "See! Look! You are my mirror!"

When we face each other, our OBPI is facing on the same side because her injury occurred on her left side and mine is on the right. "You are my sister!", I said.

I'd never met anyone in my life with OBPI in person and neither had she. I had joined BPI Facebook groups and was overly excited when I met another young woman the same age as me with OBPI who lived in the U.S.. But it's not the same as being with someone in person who shares part of your experience. Truss and I both felt alone up until that night. I started crying and

My sister, Truss, and me

Photo credit: Shakti Raph

I saw her eyes start to water. She then said "This is crazy! You're going to make me cry."

At that point I started bawling on her shoulder because I was feeling all sorts of mixed emotions. I wished my mom were alive so I could have told her what happened but I know she is looking over me and saw everything. My family was so shocked when I shared the amazing news with them.

Truss and I were complete strangers, but instantly became family. We hugged each other, cried and laughed. I couldn't wait to tell so many people. We texted each other way after the event was over still in shock at what had happened. I've been waiting on something like this my entire life! I knew it was going to happen soon enough but I was not expecting it to happen by fate right before my book was supposed to be published!

I think the craziest part of it all is that we are a year apart in age and are both "Libras"! Truss and I are both young Black women with the same physical disability and we will not allow society to define who we are as people first, regardless of the labels others apply to us.

Shakil, whenever I thank you for what you've done you're always telling me that you never really did anything. I don't think you realize the importance of you making that connection. It has impacted my life in a major way now, forever. One of the biggest reasons why you wanted me to meet Truss was because I'm still battling self-confidence and caring too much about what others think about my physical appearance. You wanted me to see her and be inspired by watching her do what she loves and being so comfortable with showing her physical disability. Your mission is beyond accomplished.

I felt confident because I was inspired by Truss and it has motivated me to show everyone who the "real" me is without questioning how I'd be looked at. This was a major life changer, so once again, thank you!

My story definitely does not end here, but I'll leave you with this for now. I've come to the realization that things just happen when they are ready to happen and publishing this book is just the beginning! There will be so much more to experience and share on my journey living with OBPI, meeting my other OBPI brothers and sisters as well as continuing to raise awareness of Brachial Plexus Injuries in general.

Be sure to reach out and stay connected!

Dear Reader,

Thank you for taking the time to read my memoir. I am overjoyed to have shared my life story thus far, with you. I hope you enjoyed it and have been touched by at least one experience of mine. As mentioned before my hope for the book was to motivate and inspire others with my life story. I hope you have a better understanding of what it is like for someone like me to be living with Obstetrical Brachial Plexus Injury and can share your knowledge with others. Writing this memoir has been so therapeutic for me and I'm definitely not done here!

I hope to have motivated or inspired you in some way and I'm always willing to hear the stories of others. Do not be afraid to reach out to me! I'd love to connect with you!

Connect with me!
Follow me on Twitter & Instagram: *@Wyn_inspires*
Email me: *wynnikka.matthews@outlook.com*

You are Amazing!
You are a STAR!
Shine bright!
Live LIFE!

Yours Truly,
Wynnikka Matthews

Photo credit: Shakil Raph

www.ingramcontent.com/pod-product-compliance
Lightning Source LLC
Chambersburg PA
CBHW070906080526
44589CB00013B/1197

* 9 7 8 1 7 7 5 0 4 2 8 0 8 *